Bruce Lindsey

Digital Gehry
Material Resistance / Digital Construction

Preface by Antonino Saggio

Birkhäuser – Publishers for Architecture
Basel • Boston • Berlin

A CIP catalogue record for this book is available from the Library of Congress, Washington D.C., USA.

Deutsche Bibliothek Cataloging-in-Publication Data

Digital Gehry: material resistance/digital construction / Bruce Lindsey. - Basel ; Boston ; Berlin : Birkhäuser, 2001
    ISBN 3-7643-6562-5

Original edition:
Digital Gehry: resistenza materiale / costruzione digitale (Universale di Architettura 104, collana fondata da Bruno Zevi; La Rivoluzione Informatica, sezione a cura di Antonino Saggio).
© 2001 Testo & Immagine, Turin

© 2001 Birkhäuser – Publishers for Architecture, P.O. Box 133, CH-4010 Basel, Switzerland.
Member of the BertelsmannSpringer Publishing Group.
Printed on acid-free paper produced from chlorine-free pulp. TCF ∞
Printed in Italy
ISBN 3-7643-6562-5

9 8 7 6 5 4 3 2 1   http://www.birkhauser.ch

Contents

To Mel

I would like to thank the people at Frank Gehry Partners, especially: Keith Mendenhall, Dennis Shelden, Craig Webb, Rick Smith, and Laura Stella. Marilee Keys, Buster Maxwell, Matt Fineout, and Thomas Kim, provided invaluable help with research, refinement and copy editing. Thanks to Laura Vellucci, and Giovanni Pellicciotta, for web research. And thanks to Nino Saggio for his passion for the subject and his support.

Flying Carpets

preface by Antonino Saggio

Frank Owen Gehry opened an efficient architecture studio in 1962. But sixteen years later, almost all at once, he overthrew the canons of his daily professionalism for a new and audacious experimentation. He began an intense research presented in 1986 at a one man show that launched him into the international spotlight. Now in 2001, his praise has become unanimous. Along with the most coveted recognitions to which an architect could aspire, dozens of constructions have followed one after the other on both sides of the Atlantic, some of them acclaimed as works that are symbols of contemporary architecture.

With the collaboration of his many traveling companions, Gehry brings together a sculptural force, a sense of shifting, jagged space, an aesthetic that reflects the turbulent evolution of society. These projects are built out of incessant experimentation with widely different materials; they encounter their spaces in a provocative and courageous manner; they present a shattering expressivity, fluid and dynamic; and finally, they communicate with the powers that finance, promote, and build the works. The many pragmatic facets of the task of designing move within the synthesis of architecture as art and not vice versa.

Gehry is an architect of "doing" (and therefore the verb that moves the action rather than the adjective that describes the results). The first verb is *Assemble*. He replaces the post-modern decorativism of the late 1960s with the only vital element of consumer society that seemed useful to him to pursue: waste, recycling, reuse. From his house in Santa Monica, a world left standing in the backyards of American houses was brought to the forefront of a new experience. He would call it *cheapscape*. The second keyword is *Space*, because the architect sees the potential of articulating public space with his buildings in a balanced play between interior and exterior. This would become the center of his operations, a center frequently occupied by new pieces of art. But, as at Loyola University in Los Angeles, *space* is also a way of studying solutions and phases of construction in order to create an active dialogue with forces outside the studio, especially the clients.

Separate is another method. In works such as the Edgemar Complex the prevailing desire is to divide the volumes to give rise to new plastic results and create animated scenes that accompany, invite and imply the movements of the public. *Soar* is another key verb for works such as the Bilbao Museum where the masses follow trajectories that energize the environment. The project is wedged into a brown area specifically chosen by the architect; *cheapscape* has become *urbanscape*. The sculptural and dynamic volumes shape not only the contact with the greater city but also the interior spaces in a sort of "hyper-functionalism", given that a museum of such astounding efficiency has never before been constructed. Finally, *Liquefy*. In the latest version of the Lewis house (or the Experience Music Project in Seattle), interior and exterior, space and volumes, atmosphere and material, are now all conceived in a fluid, continuous movement: an underwater, liquid feeling emerges.

Gehry and his studio generate dozens and dozens of models. He creates in rapid sketches and in subsequent drafts shapes the material, tests the spaces, the three-dimensional effects, the play of hollows and solids. Once a satisfying model has been built, it can then be digitized (i.e. recorded in grid points with a sort of electronic pantograph) and a new model built, this time electronic, that will then become the basis for thousands of other verifications and modifications.

Naturally, there can be infinite new three-dimensional visions; new diagrams and sections can be drawn-up; every aspect of the entire project can be studied contemporaneously in minute detail. But an electronic model is by its nature something extremely different with respect to a traditional model since it is a living, interacting (and in certain aspects "intelligent") whole. While in one case the information is static, in the other all bits of information are *dynamically* interconnected. An architectural element can be modified and the effect simultaneously verified not only on the desired designs but also building codes, costs, static calculations or thermal distribution. We can verify the effects of one material with respect to another not only in its quantitative aspects but also in terms of how it reacts to natural or artificial light. Information can then be sent to those constructing the building (perhaps using equipment connected to the computer) who can then calculate how much material is needed in real time. The electronic model in this sense becomes a tool for studying, testing, simulating and constructing. It is no guarantee for success but for the task of designing it is the most important step forward since the discovery of perspective. Gehry "is frightened but completely aware".

Streams of Electrons

With these observations, we left Gehry five years ago; almost at the same time the "IT Revolution" series of publications began. Now, with *Digital Gehry*, brilliantly written by Bruce Lindsey, we have come to the fourteenth volume of the series. I would like to sum up as clearly as possible some of the points I feel are important in this book.

Lindsey is right to concentrate on Gehry's overall work methods since the innovation produced in his studio through digital practices comes from them. The reader will find detailed descriptions of the building process never disconnected from the aesthetic tension that the architect pursues or the digital methods at times used to pursue it; a combination of craft and knowledge that is rightly called an "exceptionally efficient unit".

Just like any general, Gehry has his brave colonels who, though hidden to the general public, are essential in carrying out the projects. Lindsey speaks frequently with them and brings out, almost as if in a live recording, observations, ideas and small anecdotes: thus we discover that the legendary CATIA program arrived in the studio thanks to a "corporate garage sale" at IBM, or that at the beginning of the 1990s they had only three broken-down workstations, or the role of the Italian firm Permasteelisa, or the processes involved in the concrete realization of the digital model. The chapter that narrates the development of the Fish in Barcelona, the first project of the studio actually guided by the computer, is very exciting and brilliantly written.

Lindsey also touches on conceptually important points. The first is one he defines as *Skin in*. If the modernist process begins from the structural grid toward the outside, Gehry's process is the opposite: from the shape of the skin and therefore the exterior surface, he passes to the secondary plans and structure and then to the shaping of the spaces. Let's consider the consequences of this approach. Does this "skin in" process bring with it a radically different method with respect to the "industrial" and "modernist" approach? Naturally, the reader should think about this a bit before proceeding with the following lines.

The answer is: yes, and how! The "skin in" approach is linked to a paradigmatic change in architecture as a whole. The modernist method was similar to an assembly line: pieces were developed that made up the machine/architecture, components were standardized and the various systems (of the structure, plants, exterior panels) were made as autonomous and independent as possible. Remember Le Corbusier's 5 points? The system was summarizing, mechanical and absolute. Instead, Gehry's method is "relational"; the secret is the relation between the parts instead of their independence. Underneath the curves of his architecture, the components of the construction are connected to each another through an electronic model also realized in coordinated layers; one that regards the exterior surfaces, one of wire that describes the geometry and structural grid and a third that outlines the interior cables. Together they form a sort of carpet: waving, electronic and, if we recall the Futurist, Boccionian trajectories we have used to describe his work, in flight. Streams of luminous electrons seem to trace hyperbolas in the atmosphere.

Star Dust

Everything is fine up to this point. Gehry is at the cutting-edge; his studio produces top level innovations; Gehry is incredibly successful. But luckily there is also much for others to do. In order to understand at least one direction, we must concentrate on the problem of representation, one to which Bruce Lindsey dedicates several important pages in this book.

We are accustomed to representing architecture that is already built. To designing (or measuring) the pyramids or a Renaissance palace to put back on paper something we know as a real object already existing in space. But have we ever asked ourselves the reverse? In other words, whether and to what extent a real object might "resemble" the method that its contemporaries had of representing it? Perhaps this question would reveal the fact that it is knowledge itself that is "represented" in the architectural object.

The basic rules of trigonometry are illustrated in the pyramids; a calculation based on geometry (and not the tiring Roman numerals I, II, III, IV) is at the basis of the Pantheon; the loss of geometrical-arithmetical ability is evident in the cavernous and unsteady interior of a Romanesque church; without the lines and rules of perspective there would be no "ordered" Renaissance palace, and without the circles of a compass, the curves of San Carlino or Sant'Ivo would never have taken shape. Finally, if we "also" consider the tool, we get a clue to understanding how certain senses of space were born.

Now let us try to question our ideas of architecture "together" with the tool we have with us. And let us ask ourselves, "What if our architecture were to resemble even more the potential of our computerized models?" We would like the flexibility, intelligence, speed and, as we have said many times before, interactivity of our digital model to be the special quality of constructed architecture. A property not just of our computer screens but of our architecture, constructed exactly just as the measured, ordered and centered concept of perspective led to an architecture "in its own likeness and image".

Now, by studying the architecture and process of Gehry, we understand that we are only at the beginning of this journey. Gehry's architecture resembles his sketches more and more. But the electronic model is much more; it grasps the possibility of an intelligence, a mutation, a change much much greater than that of interpreting, even though brilliantly, the symbols and dreams of a genius.

Digital Gehry was written after first hand research into the studio that is among the world's most advanced centers of architectural, structural and digital research. The small book you hold in your hands was possible thanks to the great generosity of Frank Owen Gehry and the collaboration of the many architects (and scientists and inventors) on his team. In his skillful, keen and participatory writing style, Lindsey reveals and gives examples of the fact that there can be no cutting-edge architectural research today that is not also research into information technology. But at the same time these architects "born with the computer" cannot let down their guard. We are only at the beginning of the creation of a new alphabet. And there is a great task ahead of us all.

www.arc.uniroma1.it/saggio

Numbers

In 1996 the *New York Times* established a web based searchable index that covers every word in every article written for the newspaper since that date. It is a barometer of cultural activity on a par with the Nielsen Box that rates the popularity of TV shows across the country and the ever increasing number of hamburgers sold by MacDonald's which now no longer appears on the sign because of the enormity of the number. A lot of people read the *New York Times* because it can tell us something about the current situation through the articles published. "God", for instance, shows up 14,971 times in articles published since 1996. In comparison, "Bill Clinton" registers 25,500 hits while "McDonald's" appears 53 times. "Architecture", showing a solid increase in each of the last five years, registers 7,084 hits not accounting for the ubiquitous use of the word to refer to structures in computer programming rather than buildings. Therefore architecture is clearly more important than McDonald's but has a long way to go to compete with God. Bill Clinton is big with the *New York Times*.

Following God, Frank Gehry shows 458 hits edging out Richard Meier at 312, and soundly beating Peter Eisenman at 128. Lagging only behind the dead Frank Lloyd Wright at 623, and the enduring Phillip Johnson at 1013, Frank Gehry stands as one of the most important architects of the century – or at the very least, since the 1996 beginning date of the *New York Times* index.
When I visited his Santa Monica office in November of 2000 there were 30-35 active worldwide projects being developed on two floors with 125 architects and 15 administrative people who call the boss "Frank" (not Mr. Wright).
In the recent book *Frank O. Gehry The Complete Works* (1998) by Francesco Dal Co and Kurt Forster the bibliography cites 255 projects beginning with his Senior Thesis Project at the University of Southern California in 1954 and ending with the Condé Nast Cafeteria project in New York City in 1997. The bibliography from this book also cites 1,668 articles, publications and books from 1963 to October of 1997 with writings by prominent architects,

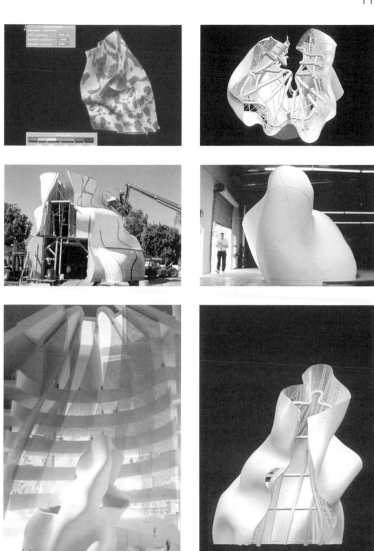

Architectural Study 2001. Top: CATIA models. Middle: fiberglass construction. Bottom: Guggenheim, New York installation rendering, CATIA model with structure.

critics and cultural observers such as: Jean-Louis Cohen, Beatriz Colomina, Francesco Dal Co, Kurt Forster, Charles Jencks, Herbert Muschamp, and Michael Sorkin, among others.

He was the 11th recipient of the Pritzker Prize in 1989. The 2001 retrospective show of Gehry's work at the Guggenheim Museum in New York City, which includes 36 projects, in 24 cities, and 5 countries, marks an important milestone in his work but in no way signals a pause or reduction in the quantity or significance of the work of Frank Gehry and his office.

In fact, at the age of 72, and as suggested by his partner Jim Glymph, they are out to change the game.

The game Glymph is referring to is nothing less than the way that architecture is practiced and the role that the architect assumes in "the most dangerous and least predictable endeavors one can still pursue in contemporary society" (Willis); namely the making of buildings.

Part of this change is being precipitated by the use of digital tools including computers, computer-aided design (CAD) software, computer aided manufacturing (CAM) techniques, and network-based communications allowing for a powerful collaborative community – all of this despite Frank Gehry's self-proclaimed "illiteracy" with and skepticism of computers.

This book will focus on Frank Gehry's evolving design process, and how digital tools and processes have been adapted to a global/collaborative/singular practice; a *fluent practice*. It will describe the organization of Gehry's office and its associated teams, and it will outline the role of digital tools in an emergent design and construction process where a renewed passion, desire, and collaboration is resulting in "a new architecture" and the reestablishment of the architect as "master builder."

> Architects hide behind the functions and the budgets and the building regulation and the gravity and the client and the time… That is a cop-out! People excuse themselves of their responsibility because they're lazy or because they don't have any talent or ideas. I have to solve all those problems, but then what? What do you do? (Zaera 1995)

Guggenheim Museum, New York, final design model. Bottom left, design process model (photos: author).

Pre:text

Before you can actually build a boat, you must loft its lines to full size. This means taking the small scale plans of the design and projecting them to actual boat size. Most boat hulls are complexes of curved surfaces. Lofting guarantees that these curves flow smoothly into one another with fair even lines… In many ways, it allows you to mentally build the boat without yet sawing any timber. Thought and head scratching expended at this stage will surely save frustration and errors after the actual construction has begun. (Gougeon 1979)

There is a beautiful process in the making of a cedar strip canoe called lofting. Lofting in generic terms is used to describe the full-scale drawing of the curves associated in the building of a boat hull or an airplane wing. It is similar to "setting out", a process that has been practiced by stone carvers for centuries. Setting out involved the full scale drawing of templates onto zinc plates. These zinc "molds" were cut out and used in the carving process much like a tailor uses a pattern. The science of stereotomy, the art of drawing and cutting solids precisely, was practiced by carvers as early as the 13th century. Using the developing science of descriptive geometry, carvers projected the shape of a three-dimensional stone, onto a two-dimensional zinc plate. Contemporary three-dimensional computer modeling programs are a direct descendent of this tradition that bridged science and art. In the loft drawing of a boat, the setting out of the transverse mold sections, usually seven in number, are augmented by several longitudinal sections that include the waterline. For a cedar strip canoe the longitudinal sections are drawn with a piece of cedar the exact dimensions anticipated for the construction, usually 10 feet long and less that an inch in its thickest dimension. The strip is bent, and traced along its edge, to produce a curve that directly utilizes the cedar's material and geometrical properties. A curve too pronounced results in the resounding "snap" of the strip. The drawing itself embodies a material memory that prefigures the construction. The drawing is built.

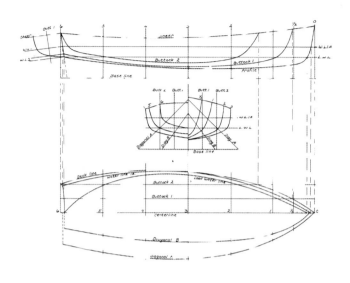

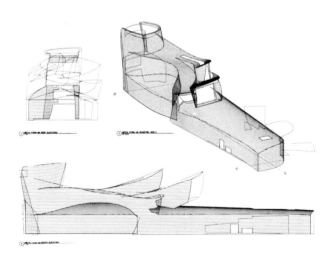

Top: boat loft drawing. Bottom: Guggenheim Museum, Bilbao, Spain, CATIA model.

1. Drawings and Models

Painting is the most marvelous, elaborate and complete way of making up my mind. (Michael Andrews)

An architect's design process comes under scrutiny only when it results in something banal or extraordinary. When the result is typical, the *process* is never an issue. In the first case when something terrible is produced, the process is elevated to an effort worthwhile in its own right, separate from the outcome (at least in the mind of the architect), least the entire endeavor be seen as a waste of time. The process becomes an exercise, or an uncontrollable force with a life of its own – this despite the likelihood that a bad outcome is the result of a bad process. This rationalization is illustrated in the adage, "experience is what you get when you didn't get what you wanted". When the result is something extraordinary it must be the result of a design process that is unique, unorthodox, magical, or idiosyncratic, and at the very least outside normative practices. Perhaps, even stemming from the practices of alchemists or artists, who as Frank Gehry describes, have the more difficult job:

I think that the painter has the most difficult problem: the white canvas and a paintbrush and a bunch of colors. How do you make the first mark. (Zaera 1995)

Norten Residence, 1982-84, model (photos: author).

A painting is an answer to a question that is posed by the painting itself. It does not suffer the same need for justification within the process of its making as architecture does. Architectural design, like painting, is a process of *making up your mind*. The products of the process, usually drawings and models, are not only rhetorical evidence of, and essential to, these decisions, but give weight, and evidence, to the choice. Drawings and models are also one of the last vestiges of the architect as builder. Contemporary architects, working at a distance, do not construct buildings; they make drawings and models. These products, which often times become significant in their own right, as is the case with Gehry's drawings, become the only way for the architect to actually "build".

Drawings and models become analogues of construction. They precede the building and are often referred to as tools. Perhaps this is due to their distance from the actual thing being developed, but likely it is due to a more fundamental difference. George Kubler in his book *The Shape of Time* sheds some light on this:

> Although a common gradient connects use and beauty, the two are irreducibly different: a tool is always intrinsically simple […] but a work of art […] is always intrinsically complicated however simple its effect may seem. (Kubler 1962)

Drawings and models (the tools) are by necessity simple and incomplete in relation to the actual building. For either to replicate the actual building (the work of art) is impossible and undesirable.

Norten Residence, 1982-84, drawing,

The drawing's simplicity – its abstraction – is a way of controlling complexity. At the same time it allows for interpretation that anticipates the future experience of the building's user. The architect uses drawings, models, and their construction, to project this future experience through a perception-in-action, or peripatetic analogy. The degree of this abstraction is controlled by the architect through the form of the modeling: two-dimensional, three-dimensional (now even four-dimensional), and also through the specificity of the depiction. By allowing the perception of the model to involve less interpretation, the model can become a method of "conventional" communication. This communication – often to the client – operates as an extension of perception. Michael Polanyi in his book *Personal Knowledge* describes beautifully how this happens for a blind person extending their sense of touch to allow them to "see" through the cane. Polanyi goes on to describe that this act of perception is only possible by becoming less (subsidiarily) aware of the vibrations through the cane, and attending to the global (focal) awareness of "seeing". If you focus on seeing, the cane becomes a vehicle for an extension of perception – if you focus on the representation, and not the cardboard or ink, so does the model or drawing.

At times the degree of abstraction, particularly for architectural drawings, may only be intelligible to the maker of the drawing. The role of these drawings is to maximize the possible interpretations. Finding the degree of abstraction required to produce an isomorphic, or corresponding potential, to some aspect of the problem, form, or site, is part of the skill of the designer. The drawing becomes not so much an act of communication, as a search for possible correspondences. With more specific drawings, come more predictable implications. The more abstract the drawing, the more likely it may provoke correspondences that could not have been predicted in advance.

Drawings and models provoke certain actions and resist others. Drawings and models offer different possibilities for change. Models, which tend to emphasize the totality of a situation due to their small size, encourage rearrangement. The pieces can be moved. They also allow for concentrated or widespread alteration. They are more specific than drawings and exist in space as we do. They can resist spontaneity due to the time and intention required to build them. Drawings, on the other hand, are usually

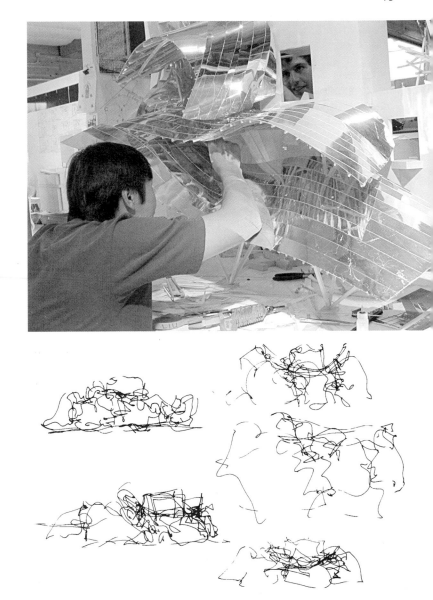

Top: Marques de Riscal Winery, El Ciego, *Spain, 1998, design process model. Bottom:* Experience Music Project, *1995-2000, Seattle, WA, drawings (photo: author).*

perceived as fragments of larger wholes. Drawings, while much faster than models in keeping up with thought, are more susceptible to redrawing than alteration. Drawings promote small and numerous changes to be evaluated through time. Drawings are a recording of perception where the distance from the hand to the brain is shortened.

Drawing and modeling is a way of thinking out loud – we represent things in ways that are related to how we think. We think in words, sounds, pictures, images, and more recently, in photographs, movies, morphs, and webs. We also conceive of new things using these modes of representation and thinking. The circularity of this relationship underpins the capacity for these representations to embody a kind of embedded theory: how we depict the world can actually effect how we think about, and see the world. A historical example of this is the well-documented change in perception due to the rediscovery of linear perspective by Brunelleschi at the beginning of the Renaissance.

In this way, the products of the design process are not neutral and have the capacity to engage larger cultural implications. It is also likely that as we have invented new ways to represent things, so to, have we prompted new ways of conceiving of things.

> So the organizing move of the artist is merely displaced from the hand on the paintbrush to the finger on the shutter. And in that instant of framing, the old culture-creatures re-emerge from their lair, trailing the memories of generations behind them. (Schama 1995)

Ray and Maria Stata Center, MIT, Cambridge, MA. Final design model in Gehry's office (photo: author).

2. Gehry's Process BC (Before Computers)

Trained in an era when becoming an architect was an "act of social responsibility" (Jencks), Gehry was forty-nine years old and had been practicing architecture for sixteen years when he designed his own house in Santa Monica, California in 1978. It brought him international attention. Since the beginning he has been articulate about his design process, and how it has evolved through a conscious "honing of his visual intellect", and an acute visual memory (Ivy 1999). When asked how he starts a project, Gehry replies, "through drawing". When asked where he gets his ideas, he states, "we talk to the client, a lot". Kubler writes:

> We still see [...] genius as a congenital disposition and as an inborn difference of kind among men, instead of as a fortuitous keying together of disposition and situation into an exceptionally efficient entity. (Kubler 1962)

These self-effacing comments by Gehry himself, and the tendency of others to dismiss his hard work to the exigency of genius, hide the "exceptionally efficient entity" of his design process. Similarly the designation of Gehry as an artist, and his work as sculptural, has inexplicably delayed the recognition that he and his office deserve in contributing to changes in architecture and architectural practice. His matter-of-fact manner also hides the obvious importance of the statements themselves – he does begin a project through drawing, and he does talk "a lot" to his clients.

Davis Studio and Residence, Malibu, 1972, CA, drawing.

2.1 Drawing

However, Gehry's confidence in the drawing and the client was not always evident. In the early sixties, having just opened his own office, he began to be suspicious of the capacity of drawings to distract his attention from the building by being "glib" or superficial. This suspicion did not stem from a lack of technique. Trained in architectural rendering, and practicing early in his career for architect John Portman, Gehry was a very capable draftsman. In addition, his early professional work with Hideo Sasaki, Pereira & Luckman, and later with Victor Gruen Associates, ranged from housing to retail projects. It was Victor Gruen who influenced Gehry the young intern to return to school at Harvard in 1956 to study urban planning – a key event for Gehry's growing belief in the importance of architecture's connection to the city. He came to believe that drawings, which emphasized the "drawing", could not reveal these possible connections. He was prompted to try an unorthodox method that would characterize his belief in the generative capacity of the drawing. He began to have his structural engineer draft the plan and elevation drawings so that he could concentrate on the *building* through his own kind of drawing:

> I do a different kind of drawing [than the structural engineer]. They are a searching in the paper. It's almost like I'm grinding into the paper, trying to find the building. It's like a sculptor cutting into the

Third Army Day Room Improvements, Fort Bragg, NC, early sketch by Gehry, 1956.

23

stone or the marble, looking for the image. […] It's a frantic kind of searching. I let that lead, and then make models of the idea scratched out of the paper, and then go back to the drawing and so on. (Arnell, Bickford 1985)

In his essay "The Contradictions Underlying the Profession of Architecture" in the book *The Emerald City*, Dan Willis describes the problematic belief that a contemporary architect's working drawings are complete but abstract representations of buildings. This results in architecture that looks like built drawings.

The logic of the drawing has superseded the logic of building, resulting in buildings that aspire to be like drawings […] during construction, the uninhibited freedom of such drawings will often translate into a building that is very difficult to construct, and so the logic of the building stands in direct contradiction to the logic of the drawing that inspired it. (Willis 1999)

This belief, combined with the legal necessity for drawings to represent a complete building, prevents the necessary translation and improvisation from the architect's design through the construction that results in a fluent work of architecture. Gehry himself describes this problem when he states:

For example, Michael Graves' first drawings are beautiful, but he can never make a building that is as beautiful as the drawing […]. I always focus on the building; the drawings are not important to me; they are just stepping-stones. And they do not even look like the building, but I know what they are telling me to do next. (Zaera 1995)

2.2 Models
One of the ways that Gehry focuses on the building is by translating the drawing into a physical model. This crucial step relates the drawing to the "logic" of construction missing in the sequence described by Willis. The model, existing in space, is less abstract than the drawing and is made from actual materials. The "material resistance" provided by paper, cardboard, copper, or other stuff, recalls the use of cedar in the lofting of a strip canoe. The behavior of the material, while not the same as the actual material of construction, still provides a tactile feedback that facilitates

and resists certain formal arrangements. This might result in a building that looks like a model instead of a drawing, were it not for Gehry's unwavering attention to the instrumental role of both. This material resistance is missing when building virtual models in a computer – an important influence on Gehry's skepticism to the adaptation of digital tools.

Another dimension of this material resistance is related directly to the immediacy of working with materials themselves rather than an abstraction. Gehry describes the process of working on the Easy Edges furniture line in the late sixties and early seventies as "some of the most rewarding times of my life". Because of the kinesthetic unmediated and physical process, the furniture, made from corrugated cardboard, embodied the energy and spontaneity of a material research, coupled with a joy of building. It would characterize a long term working method through the architectural model.

Gehry's use of the model also follows as a direct response to his desire to work with the client. For those not trained to read drawings, models are much easier to understand. They are three-dimensional. They envision space. They are miniature buildings. The use of the model allows the client to participate in the dialogue of the process. Like the drawing, they

Easy Edges Furniture, 1979-1982 (photo: author).

can be operated on, and because they are incomplete, as all representations are, they require an active perceptual spatial participation. The need for the client to see the space was an important requirement.

> For me [Gehry] the most distinctive quality of architecture with respect to other practices is the fact that it encloses space. (Zaera 1995)

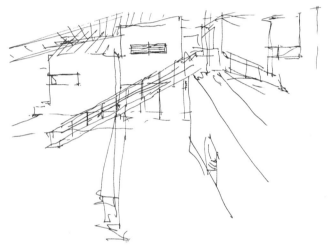

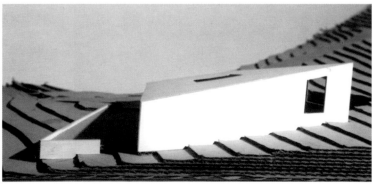

Davis Studio and Residence, Malibu, CA 1972, interior sketch and site model.

In the Davis House and Studio in Malibu, California of 1972, the use of strings on the site model describing perspectival lines above the terrain allowed for a direct manipulation of the proposed space by moving the strings; Gehry's intention being to connect the building to the work of client Ron Davis who used and manipulated perspective methodically in his paintings. While Gehry admitted that "he [Gehry] didn't need the strings to see it" and "he [Davis] never got it", it illustrates the operative and exploratory capacity of the model that in this case resulted in a building embodying "perspectival space".

Because of this operative capacity, the models often have the look of being thrown together or casually made, belying their actual "use" as an object through which experimentation occurs. The models are built, rebuilt, torn apart and modified ruthlessly often requiring a more polished one to be made for formal presentations to the client. Plan and section drawings convey the functional aspects of the project, which Gehry describes as:

> An intellectual exercise. That is a different part of the brain. It's not less important, it's just different. And I make a value out of solving all these problems, dealing with the context and the client and finding my moment of truth after I understand the problem. (Gehry, Futagawa)

Another use of the model in Gehry's early process may relate to a prominent project: the Danzinger Studio located in Los Angeles

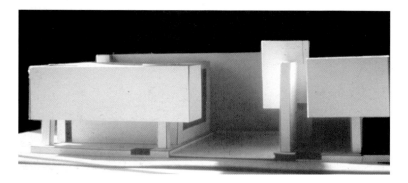

Danzinger Studio and Residence, Hollywood, CA, 1964-65, model.

and dating from 1964-65. The minimalist stucco composition of volumes was a skillful late modernist composition. Knowing the importance of the color and texture of the stucco walls Gehry built full-scale mock-ups to extend the models research – a part of his process that continues to be important today. Despite an attempt to relate the house to the street, Gehry felt it failed to make larger connections to the city. The building did not engage the context in a way that could contribute to its own complexity.

> The Danzinger Studio was an attempt to create a marginal, controlled world within the messiness of the LA urban environment. When I did it, everybody was very impressed, but I realized that neglecting a potential interface with the city was a very limiting attitude. After this project, I became much less moralistic about LA and more interested in developing a productive relationship between my architecture and the city. (Zaera 1995)

This desire to engage the larger context was limited by the small scale of the projects that the office was working on in the late seventies and early eighties. Coupled with a desire to break the program into discrete pieces a new direction began to manifest itself as small block planning, using "juxtaposed pavilions of one-room buildings", that Charles Jencks cites as one of the four new ideas that Gehry has brought to architecture.

Gehry Residence, Santa Monica, CA, model (photo: author).

The other three are "perspective space", as illustrated in the Davis Studio; the use of "cheap *démodé* materials in a creative way", demonstrated in Gehry's own house; and a search "into a new language of curved forms", that continues to evolve in his current work.

The urban inspired small block planning strategy was fully exploited in the multi-phase Loyola University Law School project beginning in 1978. By fragmenting the project program into single buildings, a city-like composition was developed. This resulted in an arrangement of spaces that created a sense of emergent community for the university commuters in the car-scape of Los Angeles.

Urban designers have long used block models to describe and understand the scale and space of the city. The order of the city is a result of the particularity of each piece or building arrayed across a field of attraction. A whole emerges from the connections of the individual pieces. The individuality of the model pieces provokes new arrangements and again the operative capacity of the model allows for new interpretations. Another reading of the Loyola "model' is as a three-dimensional bubble diagram (Sorkin, Dal Co) of functionally specific and spatially suggestive relationships. This concept finds a place in Gehry's later work as color-coded block models that precede the explosive phase of the design. Here the urban planning city block model is compressed into a single building model where the individual blocks prompt

 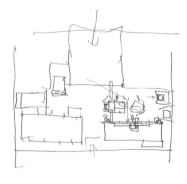

Loyola University, Law School, Los Angeles, CA, 1978-, model and sketch (photo: author).

re-arrangement. These parts also allow the client to have multiple points of reference and possibilities for interpretations. In this way the models operate much like the Renaissance Memory Theatres where objects in an elaborate stage are associated with dialogue to be remembered. Gehry sees these multiple readings as a way for the building to escape becoming obsolete. His re-arrangement of the blocks and the persistent alteration and addition through multiple iterations continues to be an important part of his design process.

2.3 Collaboration
Design tends to be a habitual practice. Perhaps this is due to the complexity, and difficulty of architectural problems with their broadly based cultural, artistic, and scientific implications. It more likely is due to human nature where we tend to do those things that we know we can do. Partly due to this tendency, and also because of the sheer fun of it, collaboration is a very important part of Gehry's process. It allows him to provoke his typical instincts with another eye and hand. It is a way of expanding his instincts, with a humane practice that challenges the authority of individual practice through creative collisions. Gehry states, in reference to his work with Lucinda Childs and John Adams, for the stage set of the 1983 dance performance *Available Light*:

Ray and Maria Stata Center, 1998- MIT, Cambridge, MA, Program model (photo: Whit Presten).

> We wanted to make something that none of us would have done alone. That is the essence of collaboration. When you agree to collaborate, you agree to jump off a cliff holding hands with everyone, hoping the resourcefulness of each will insure that you all land on your feet. (Walker Art Center 1986)

While Gehry's influence by, and collaboration with artists, is well known, the Camp Good Times project of 1984-1985 exemplifies his belief in collaboration. The camp, a retreat for children with cancer, was to be built in the Santa Monica Mountains. Gehry took the project with the condition that artists, Claes Oldenburg, Coosje van Bruggen, and landscape architect Peter Walker, be a part of the design team. With help from fifteen architecture students from Harvard, and the camp director, the team in response

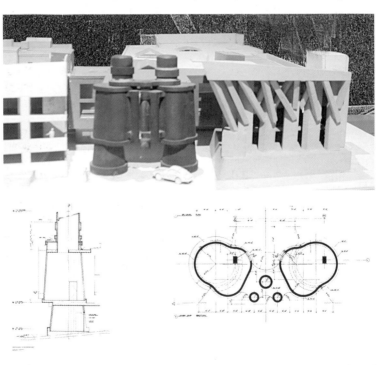

Chiat Day Building, Venice, CA, 1985-91, design process model, plan and section (photo: author).

to the dry, arid, and hot climate of the site developed a series of water and maritime inspired buildings. An upside down skeleton of a ship hull provided the entrance canopy to the dining hall, which had a roof formed of frozen wave shapes. A bridge designed by van Bruggen, and a milk can shaped kitchen, ("the ancient Ravenna chapel-like milk can kitchen) showing the influences of Oldenburg's large scale sculptures surrounded the main public space. Gehry says of the shapes that were intended to be playful, "[we] arrived at a form that grew out of our collaboration in a very natural way". He goes on to describe the development of forms that were between "abstractions and things" to be key to the collaboration. In the end, the client (a famous actor) went for a *Huckleberry Finn* atmosphere with log cabins, and the design team resigned so as not to delay the construction of the project. Later in the Chiat / Day project in Venice, CA, of 1985-91 Gehry would team up with Oldenburg and van Bruggen again for the design of the famous Binocular entrance piece. The interior of the building was originally intended to be designed by ten artists but ended up with two conference rooms designed by Mike Kelly. Finding out "what would happen if an artist were really a part of the building process" inspired Gehry and further collaborations.

Camp Good Times, Santa Monica Mountains, CA, 1984-85, final design model.

3. Barcelona Fish: A Digital Collusion

Col·lu·sion [ke loozh'n] noun
secret cooperation: secret cooperation between people in order to do
something illegal or underhanded

When Jim Glymph joined Frank Gehry's office in 1989 there were
only two computers and both were in accounting (Cocke 2000).
Glymph came to the office, in part, due to the difficulty that
Gehry faced in realizing the Disney Concert Hall. The office
worked with French aerospace engineers who helped design the
Mirage fighter. They developed a computer model of a doubly
curving stone panel of the concert hall exterior. The model was
used to generate tool paths that automated the carving process
and demonstrated the feasibility of the process. Despite this
graphic proof showing that the complex forms could be constructed economically, the project was plagued by budget over-
runs. In a manner typical of many architectural offices, Gehry produced design documents that were subsequently developed by
another firm designated as the Executive Architect. Almost ten
years later, the building now under construction with a metal skin
– Gehry describes the difficulty:

> We redid the working drawings completely from scratch because the
> former executive architect was not capable of doing them. You
> couldn't build our building from his drawings… They wanted to do it
> in the way they always did it. (Ivy 1999)

Glymph, with extensive experience as an Executive Architect,
began to develop the in-house expertise to realize the increasingly
exuberant formal developments of Gehry. A "technical genius,"
as described by Gehry, Glymph immediately saw the deeper
potential for the computer to assist in the construction of the
more complex shapes. The first real test would come in a building
for the 1992 Olympic Village in Barcelona – part of a residential
and commercial masterplan designed by Bruce Graham of
Skidmore Owings and Merrill (SOM). The 54-meter-long and 35-
meter-high fish-shaped canopy was part of a 14,000 square
meter commercial development designed by Gehry. The dynamic
shape was to be realized in a steel frame clad in woven stainless

Vila Olympica, Barcelona, Spain, 1989-92, physical model, site model (photo: author).

34

steel. With an extremely tight construction schedule of ten
months, Glymph faced a familiar architectural problem – how to
build a complex object, in a short amount of time, within the
budget allotted.
The design was initially developed from Gehry's sketches and
translated into a wood and metal model. With the design work
complete, the problem emerged: how to construct and support a
fish. Glymph and the office worked with William Mitchell,
Professor of Architecture and computer guru at Harvard, and stu-
dent Evan Smythe to model the complex form with Alias software. They produced a digital model that was visually accurate
but lacked the necessary surface information to construct the
form. The surface of the Alias computer model, defined as a grid
of polygons approximating the shape, did not allow for the precise spatial location of points on the surface. The majority of the
software written for the architectural field at the time consisted of
either two-dimensional drafting programs or modeling programs
designed for visualization. This software could not support the
connection of the digital model to computer aided manufacturing
that Glymph felt was an essential step in building the complex
forms.

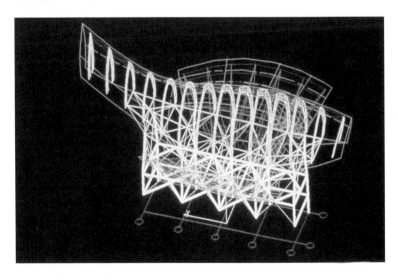

Vila Olympica, Barcelona, Spain, 1989-92, CATIA model.

Knowing that the software that could produce the required accuracy and depth existed in the automotive and aerospace industry, Glymph went searching for the right application. He found it in CATIA, a software suite developed for the aerospace industry by Dassault, a French software company associated with IBM. He also found something else – Rick Smith.

> The idea was Jim Glymph's. He contacted me at my office. I was working for IBM at the time. They said they wanted to build a building in the shape of a fish. You know we're in the aerospace industry and we we're all kind of laughing, but I liked the idea. I could take this on... I always wanted to be an architect. (Smith in Lindsey 2000)

In 1991 during a downturn in the aerospace industry Smith hired on to Gehry's office as a consultant. He speculates that his provisional role stemmed from Gehry's skepticism of computers that took three years to overcome. Equipped with an old workstation and a copy of CATIA he purchased from IBM in a "corporate garage sale", Smith began to develop a digital model of the fish. Using methods previously employed by Gehry's office to produce the tedious hand done drawings; string, plumb bobs, and countless measurements, a digital model was produced. It was based on CATIA's complete numerical control, developing descriptions for the surface that were described by polynomial equations. The surface was literally "built" using the mathematical equations of descriptive geometry. This allowed the spatial location of any point on the surface to be determined precisely. Smith's digital model was used to directly generate a laser-cut paper stack model that was compared to the original physical model in order to verify the accuracy of the translation. It matched.

Working from the surface of the digital model Smith developed a series of connection points that located where the woven skin could be attached to the steel frame. These points were converted to AES format and used by the structural engineers of SOM to develop the structural skeleton. The skin was offset from the structure an average of 10" and was supported from the frame with steel strakes of varying sizes. This system – a skin, a space for connection, and a space for the structure – anticipated the systems later used on the Guggenheim Museum in Bilbao (1991-97), and the Experience Music Project (EMP) in Seattle (1995-2000).

36

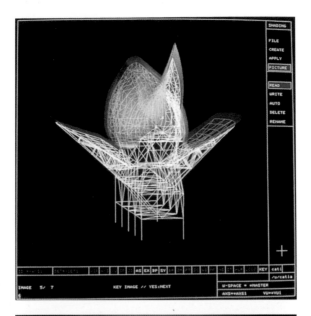

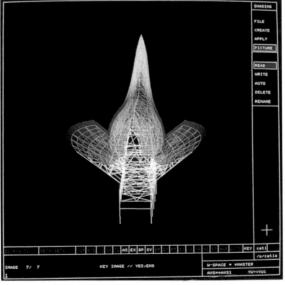

Vila Olympica, Barcelona, Spain, 1989-92, CATIA models.

Working from the "skin in" is a common practice in the automotive industry where large clay models are developed, digitally modeled, and used as the spatial envelope for the development of the structure – an ironic twist with respect to the Disney Concert Hall, where the flower-like exterior forms were an attempt by Gehry to outwardly express the acoustically driven interior space.

Beginning the construction from the digital model, Massimo Colomban's Italian firm Permasteelisa, known for their innovative work on such projects as the glazing for the Sydney Opera House, produced a traditional set of carefully dimensioned working and structural drawings. As part of their construction contract they were obligated to produce a full-size mock-up to demonstrate the

Vila Olympica, Barcelona, Spain, 1989-92, top right and bottom (photo: Laura Lee).

construction methods and allow for modifications. Working from the structure to the skin, and hampered by the difficulty of understanding a complex three-dimensional form with two-dimensional drawings, they failed six times (Novitski 1992).

Smith flew to Italy and, for eleven days, worked with the construction team to "get it out". Working from the skin to the structure, "form follows skin", they determined the exact dimensions of each strake and produced paper templates that were used to cut and bend each piece. It worked. A new lofting process was invented – one based on a digital collusion.

Realizing the value of this process, Permasteelisa immediately bought a CATIA workstation and in collaboration with the architects produced the information that allowed the project to be fabricated and constructed. Time from design to completion: six months. Glymph's describes the success of the revolutionary process; "of the thousands of connections two were off by 3 millimeters" (Novitski).

3.1 Hanover

When Rick Smith returned from Italy, Frank Gehry was getting ready for a three-day trip to Japan. The initial work on the Disney Concert Hall was in full swing and, prompted by the success with the Barcelona fish, Gehry asked Smith to get the physical model of the Concert Hall into the computer.

> So I worked for 72 straight hours at the terminal. When he returned, he looked at it and said, "Okay, it looks like he can do it" and he walked away. And I'm dropping on the floor dead tired... It was an interesting period. It was a lot of fun. A lot of adrenaline was flowing because the architect said we need to do – this. So I would sit there and think well, either we have to invent a new technique, or we use something I've done in aerospace and apply it forward; it was a very inventive period. (Smith in Lindsey 2000)

A key reason for Gehry's adaptation of digital tools was the increasingly difficult task of describing the innovative new designs to the contractor. His complex three-dimensional forms, when represented in traditional two-dimensional plans, sections, and details appeared to be even more complex.

The Weisman Art Museum in Minneapolis (1990-1993) was the

last project to be done in Gehry's office entirely by hand. The curvilinear developments of the facade were based on sliced and tilted platonic solids, in part, to help control the complexity of the geometry. Glymph states:

> Many of the forms he is developing now are only possible through the computer […] Bilbao is a perfect example. Prior to the development of the computer applications in the office, they would have been considered something to move away from. (Zaera 1995)

Algorithmic Compressibility, a concept in computer programming, describes the ability for information to be represented in ways that are shorter than the original. A short story is a description of events that is compressed relative to the actual occurrences in time. A JPEG computer image file is smaller than its original counterpart. Compressions occur through a loss of information. This is what makes them useful. A classic example of the limitations of compressibility is conveyed in the current use of computer programs used to predict the weather through simulations. As simulations become more complete, and thorough, both in the quantity of information, and the time they take to run, they approach the complexity of the actual event. The ultimate simulation results in a model of the weather occurring in real-time, describing weather that has already occurred. The comedian Stephen Wright illustrates this when he says: "I have a map of the United States. It is full-size. I don't know where to put it". This is also part of the definition used in the Science of Complexity to describe a complex situation – one that cannot be described in any other way except through the situation itself. As Gehry's forms become more complex, it may well be that the only sufficient (geometrical) description of the form is the form itself – now as a three-dimensional digital model.

Another more direct benefit of the digital model is that the work is always proceeding in a three-dimensional design space. This logic is especially important for Gehry's complex curving forms which have few orthogonal orientations that are the starting point for most architectural drawing systems. Glymph adds that the three-dimensional information of the model is also much more useful to the contractor than the information of the traditional drawing (Zaera 1995). Ultimately the design, and the con-

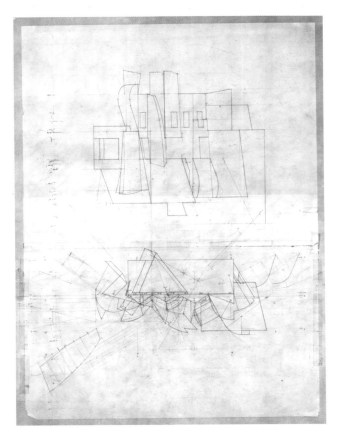

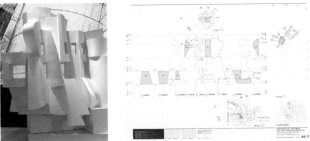

Frederick R Weisman Museum, Minneapolis, MI, 1990-93. Top: descriptive geometry drawing of facade. Bottom: facade model, working drawing (photo: author).

struction of a three-dimensional building will occur using only three-dimensional representations.

A bus stop in Hanover, Germany was the next project that allowed Gehry to push the process begun with the fish in Barcelona. One of ten architects chosen to design bus stops for Expo 2000, Gehry designed a shallow arching vault of silver and green stainless steel ribbons. Supported by a dense cluster of columns, the small project was completely developed from the CATIA model without any other kind of construction documenta-

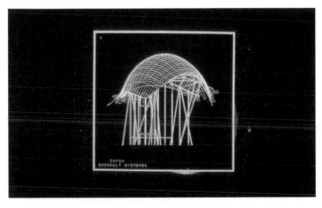

Hanover Bus Stop, Hanover, Germany, 1991-94. Top: CATIA model. Bottom: physical model (photo: Joshua White).

tion. This paper-less experiment on a manageable project provided valuable lessons for future larger-scale uses of this digitally adapted process.

3.2 Bilbao

Thomas Krens, the curator for the Guggenheim Museums, states that Gehry has "a greater faith in process than any other architect". When Gehry won the competition to design the Guggenheim Museum in Bilbao, Spain in 1991, his process was in the midst of changing from a traditional practice to a digitally adapted one.

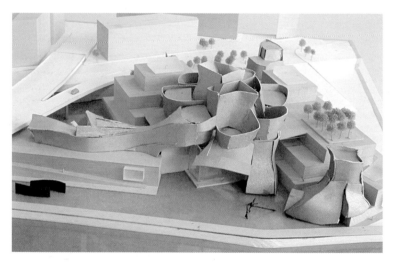

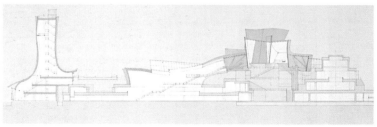

Guggenheim Museum Bilbao, 1991-97. Top: competition model. Bottom: watercolor section competition submission (photo: author).

An important event coincided with this project and Gehry's increasing use of digital tools. Randy Jefferson, an executive architect with extensive experience as a project manger, joined the team. Jefferson explains his role as "creating the important balance between excellence in design and excellence in technical development". Gehry, who describes Jefferson as a great manager, who knows how to organize a project, wanted better control of the entire process from design through construction. Jefferson turned out to be just the guy to make this happen with the Guggenheim museum.

The design team's winning competition model was accompanied by beautiful watercolor rendered plan, section, and elevation drawings – as if trying to compensate for the digital invasion brewing in the office. In fact, these drawings were done using traditional methods, as was most of the early design development for the project that lasted almost three years. Occurring at the same time as work on the Nationale-Neederlanden Building in Prague, and the Team Disneyland Administration Building, in Anaheim, California, scheduling CATIA time on one of the office's three workstations was difficult. (Fineout) Using the tried and true pre-digital methods of the office, most of the early development of the museum's complex three-dimensional form was tediously drawn by hand – descriptive geometry replacing the computer screen. It was not until the final design model was complete that the computer was extensively used. A digital model was produced in CATIA by digitizing the design model. Still unsure as to the accuracy of translation from physical model to digital model, a three-dimensional check model was

Guggenheim Museum Bilbao, 1991–97, final check model (photo: author).

produced using an automated milling machine. The milling machine took its information directly from the digital model. Verifying that the digital information was correct, the digital model became the dimensional reference that allowed the working drawings to be developed, and later helped to coordinate the construction of the project.

Gehry working with project designer Edwin Chan, Jefferson, and the design team, quickly won the confidence of the engineering team IDOM put in place to manage the Guggenheim project for Krens and the Basque government. While many local architects described the building as "not buildable", the design team gave the Basque government "proof" that they could work with budget, and time, – trust grew "exponentially". Ground breaking occurred on October 22, 1993 while the design development was still in progress. The building, a monumental, "breathing", form clad in titanium, was completed in March of 1997.

No two elements of the structure for the 24,000 square meter building are the same. One figure describes this complexity and the impossibility of organizing the project without the use of the CATIA digital model; 50,000 drawings and 60,000 hours of computing time were needed to produce the elements of the building facade.(Nicolin) The Spanish company Urssa, who used an innovative software package called BOCAD to develop shop drawings for the steel fabrication, logged much of the computing time. The steel bids for Bilbao came in at 18 percent under budget. (Ivy) At the height of the construction process 18 CATIA stations leased

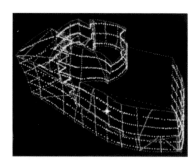 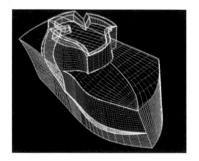

Guggenheim Museum Bilbao, 1991-97, digitizing sequence, a series of points are developed in CATIA, the points are developed into to a surface.

from aerospace contractors were being used to detail the glazing package for the museum.

The structural grid for the building is based on a steel frame, 3 meters on a side. While the steel members themselves are straight (except in the long gallery and the tower) the frames are not always parallel or orthogonal. The frames required no additional shoring to be erected. Bolted one-to-the-other, the form of the building emerged as the pre-fabricated steel frames were assembled. Off set from the frame are splines of 60mm diameter steel tubes that established the horizontal curvature. Light gauge steel studs at right angles to the splines describe the vertical curvature. The splines were connected to the frame with a uni-strut adjustable joint that Matt Fineout, project team member, describes as, "the secret to the construction of Bilbao". The joint allowed for the tuning of the splines to precisely support the titanium skin. All of the titanium cladding panels were supplied flat and four panel sizes were used for cladding 80 percent of the surface.

While much of the building component fabrication could have utilized computer aided manufacturing techniques, only the stone for the project utilized this capability. Harkening back to medieval stonecutters under a tent on the new floor of the museum, the Spanish limestone for the museum was cut using computer numerically controlled routers. The design team jokes that the museum was built without a tape measure – the "digital prosthesis" of the CATIA model providing all dimensional information (Leuyer 1997).

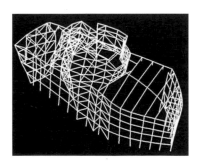

Guggenheim Museum Bilbao,1991-97. A wire frame model is developed, a check model is milled to ensure accuracy.

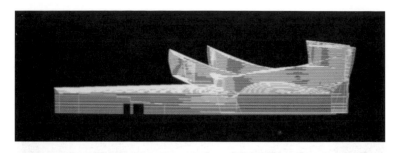

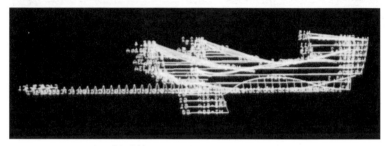

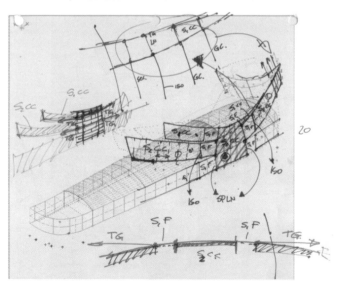

Guggenheim Museum Bilbao,1991-97. Top: CATIA model. Middle: CATIA model of splines. Bottom: notes over CATIA printout (Fineout).

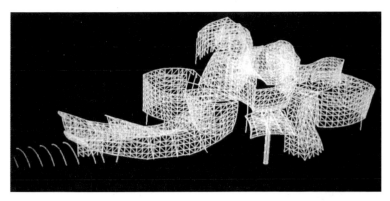

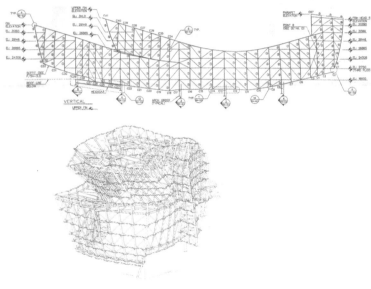

Guggenheim Museum Bilbao,1991-97. Top: CATIA model of steel frame. Middle: steel shop drawings. Bottom: computer model of steel frame for flower.

4. Gehry's Process: Digitally Adapted

I did what I always do. I picked it off the shelf and co-opted it. (Forster 1999)

The computer was introduced into Frank Gehry's office in a way that would not interfere with a design process that had been evolving for over thirty years (Zaera 1995). This reluctant assimilation was clearly contrary to the rhetoric of the eighties that surrounded digital tools and their promise to radically revolutionize not only architecture but everything else.

The revolution has been, in part, precipitated by three things: the speed of technological development as described in Moore's Law; the transmissibility of digital information breaking down traditional boundaries of time and space; and the seemingly infinite forms that information can take.

Buildings, on the other hand, are slow, immovable, site- and time-specific, singular in form, and multifarious in experience. This may be a description of Gehry's evolutionary process. On the other hand, one could say that his buildings have contributed to changing those very aspects of architecture itself. His structures are fast, move, are very recognizable wherever they are, and seemingly defy precedent due to their idiosyncrasy. Richard Sennett describes the human paradox; we fear change yet, "things that

Guggenheim Museum Bilbao, 1991-97 (photos: author).

stay the same lose their significance". Despite the efforts to the contrary, the introduction of digital tools did change Gehry's process. They also changed his architecture. Gehry had already won the Pritzker Prize in 1989 without the help of computers when Jim Glymph and Rick Smith joined the office. After they joined him, and with the help of others such as Randy Jefferson, Craig Webb, Edwin Chan, and later Dennis Shelden they designed and constructed the Guggenheim Museum in Bilbao Spain; a building heralded as the most important building of the century. It would likely have been a different building without the use of digital tools. Perhaps one that was not as fast, did not move, and did not change.

4.1 Building a Program

> We play in very neutral blocks for a long time until we get the organization on the site and the scale right. While we're doing that is when I do the sketches, because as soon as I understand the scale of the building and the relationship to the site and the relationship to the client, I start doing sketches. (Ivy 1999)

Despite the important role that computers now play in Gehry's process, the early stages still rely on models and client interaction to develop the functional relationships (architectural programming) for the project. As his projects have become larger and more complex, the importance of block models as a way of developing the architectural program have increased. These models

Ray and Maria Stata Center, 1998- MIT, Cambridge, MA, program model.

50

form a visual accounting of the numerous program elements and allow arrangement and rearrangement, suggesting both functional and spatial relationships simultaneously. Often color-coded and developed at least in two scales; one on a site model and one larger – the models become one of the first ways for the client and client team to enter the process. Working at two scales prevents myopia and seeks to avoid what Gehry describes as "the object of desire", where he becomes enamored with one possibility. Gehry states, "shifting scales forces you to be careful".

Once ascribed to a block, a program element is accounted for in the model showing the client or department representative that their particular needs are being addressed. When the model is rearranged, and the form begins to change, they can still see their piece. Taking great pleasure in getting things to function in conventional ways, Gehry does not try to fight the program so much as "re-order the priorities [...] to develop a project's potentials" (Arnell 1985). Gehry states:

This is how we move forward, and how they [the client] get what they want and feel comfortable about it... It also creates opportunities for invention, because it is the interaction that makes the process exciting and rich. (Ivy 1999)

In this early phase of the work, which proceeds slowly, plans and sections are drawn in Autocad that correspond to the block models. These plans allow functional refinements as well as preliminary budget information to be generated. The block models are augmented by maps, photographs, and surveys that allow for the site to be reconstituted in the office. For the Ohr-Okeefe Museum in Biloxi, Mississippi, a new structure located in a park filled with old-growth oak trees, a reverse topography survey was done locating the height of the tree limbs from the ground. The site model, on which the programming model is done, carefully includes the trees as well as the surrounding structures that form the context for the new building.

Depending on the type of project, consultants will be brought in to provide input and contribute to the emerging design. On larger projects, a structural engineer will be a part of the design team from the early stages developing a structural concept from the Autocad plans. When asked what happens when the structural engineer cannot figure it out, Craig Webb, a project architect that has been with Gehry for twelve years jokes: "We go get another one" (Lindsey 2000).

For the 39,000 sq. meter Ray and Maria Stata Center at the Massachusetts Institute of Technology in Cambridge (currently under construction), this phase of the process lasted over a year. It involved seven departments, twenty client representatives, and numerous user groups. The resulting arrangement of departments surrounding a courtyard reorders the program into a "sequence of neighborhoods". Strategies for the organization of the office suites drew on inspiration from sources as diverse as the behavioral patterns of orangutans, humans, and flexible arrangements inspired by traditional Japanese houses.

For the Der Neue Zollhof in Düsseldorf, a speculative office complex, Gehry arrived in Germany with a box of wood blocks, each representing 500 square meters. Gehry piled the blocks one upon the other into a single mass representing the entire 30,000 square meter program. The client, an advertising executive, Thomas Rempen stated: "Right then, we decided not to build Rockefeller

Ray and Maria Stata Center, 1998- MIT, Cambridge, MA, program model.

Center". Together they developed and built a composition of three buildings that, in Gehry's words "allows the city to breathe" (Friedman).

The numerous models exploring alternative arrangements are carefully documented using instant photographs as well as professionally shot photographs done by the resident office photographer, Whit Preston. These photographs act as a history of the process allowing previous stages to be re-captured when the design goes too far. The archive also becomes a repository of spatial types that can be used again.

After numerous block models and drawings are produced and evaluated, a final program model is completed, and the schematic design phase begins. This phase is jump-started by Gehry's gestural drawings.

4.2 Drawing and Gesture

> I do not know precisely. Sometimes it may be a kind of a gesture, an automatic reaction to some of the existing urban topographies, and inspiration from something that I have seen, a painting... My projects always develop through a succession of tests in different media that tend to evolve a gesture into a building. (Zaera 1995)

The "esquisse", as taught at the École de Beaux-Arts at the turn of the century, is a quickly done architectural drawing, usually in plan, intended to capture the essential ideas of a project's conception. French for sketch, the esquisse sets out the "parti". *Parti* from the Latin, to divide, describes the "choice, the way, the means, the method, or an attitude toward a solution" (Harbeson 1926). As the design based on the esquisse developed, often over the course of many months, the esquisse was not something from which the design of the building proceeded. Conceptually and formally complete, albeit at a preliminary stage, the esquisse was what must be *returned to*, through the laborious and iterative process of designing the building. This is a kind of "reverse engineering", where as more becomes known, and more problems are addressed, the conceptual clarity and energy of the initial gesture must be continually recaptured.

Gehry's drawings form the esquisse or a "projective argument" for a project. Taken together, all other models and drawings are a test to capture the initial gesture in a larger scale or a different material form. They also operate as a method of research where drawing engages the "visual memory", in the context of the particular project, through a kinesthetic combination of action and thought. Like Polanyi's blind person seeing through the cane, Gehry sees the project through the continuous line of the drawing. Often referring to his drawings as "scratchings", Gehry states:

> I think that way. I'm just moving the pen. I'm thinking about what I'm doing, but I'm sort of not thinking about my hands. (Van Bruggen 1997)

Drawing fast and loose is a way to keep up with the mental aberrations of a brainstorm. Abstraction multiplies interpretations. Gehry's drawings are often done in airplanes or hotel rooms – provisional states.

For the Guggenheim Museum in Bilbao, Gehry's "scratchings" were done on site. He now recalls with some surprise the "preciseness" of the early drawings in describing the form of the building that would be completed six years later. They also rely on gesture as a formal strategy. Gregg Lynn writes:

> Gestures are always intensively curvilinear. Curvilinearity signifies the principled deformation of a line while organizing many disparate elements continuously... Gestures,... are highly principled flexible connective networks. (Lynn 2001)

Gesture drawing is a common practice in *fine art* figure drawing. It is a quick, (as short as 30 seconds) active reaction to a pose attempting to capture the movement and life of the figure. This is often done first by describing the curvature of the spine as a perspectival spatial development that characterizes the position of the body in space. Recording the angle and direction of the shoulders, hips, and feet, gives the drawing the weight of the pose. When done with abandon and precision, the successful gesture drawing results in an empathetic experience: you can literally feel the pose. Gehry's drawings have this quality. Through his persistent translations in scale and material, so do his buildings. When standing in line to visit the Guggenheim Museum in Bilbao, a friend, architect Luis Rico, asked an elderly Basque woman if she liked the building.

Exclaiming that she loved it, she replied, "it feels like the wind blowing through the trees of my farm in the mountains above Bilbao".
Merce Cunningham, the great dancer and choreographer, describes bodily movement as being expressive without it needing to "mean" anything. This is because, it stems from our shared embodiedness. In a similar way the gestural empathy of Gehry's buildings escape an abstractness that allow them to "feel" familiar, despite the fact that we have never seen buildings like this before. A similar effect is produced in the work of Richard Serra, a longtime friend and collaborator of Gehry's. In Serra's large steel sculptures, the abstractness of the form and scale is countered by a material presence that is visceral. Few can stand next to one of his, sixty-foot tall, delicately balanced 2" thick steel plate sculptures, without feeling it in the stomach.

Gehry's drawings have no doubt been influenced by the degree of freedom that the computer has allowed. Knowing that complexity can be tamed using the geometry engine of CATIA, Gehry has extended the gestural qualities of his drawings. From the drawing, to the model, to the building, he describes this as his greatest strength:

> If I had to say what is my biggest contribution to the practice of architecture, I would say that it is the achievement of hand-to-eye coordination. This means that I have become very good at implementing the construction of an image or a form I am looking for. I think that is my best skill as an architect. I am able to transfer a sketch into a model into a building. (Zaera 1995)

4.3 Drawing as Provocation

Gehry's drawings play yet another critical role in the process of the design team. They precipitate the jump from one phase of the process to another in a way that is suggestive and open-ended. Because of this, they are the opposite of a diagram that seeks to clarify and be objective. Gehry's drawings seek to provoke and be intensely personal. This provocation to the project architects provides a direction not only for the evolution of the block models into the design process models, but also direction for those critical moments when the design process models jump in scale or detail. Design process models are where the development of the design occurs. This responsibility in Gehry's office lies with the project architect.

Gehry's drawings require a level of interpretation by the two primary project architects, Edwin Chan and Craig Webb. They draw on their combined experience of twenty years working with Gehry. This interpretation intensifies their different formal tendencies. Webb, project architect for the Experience Music Project (EMP) in Seattle, studied architecture at Princeton. His work tends to develop the program in colliding and interpenetrating volumes. Gehry says of him: "Craig Webb is so facile that in thirty seconds he makes something look real". Chan, project designer for the Guggenheim Museum, studied architecture at Harvard and tends towards flying surfaces and exploding shapes. Gehry describes him: "If I give Edwin Chan a sketch, he'll take it to the moon. By the time I get there he's doubled the budget" (Friedman 1991).

While these forms are suggested by Gehry's drawings they are also the result of the interaction between Gehry and his project architects. He describes the difficulty of keeping the energy of an idea alive through the countless steps, numerous people, and extended time frame of the process from design to completion. An operative strategy in his design process is to ensure a level of dynamic indeterminacy that destabilizes his own reasonable habits. Gehry states: "I try to avoid prejudices, to let my imagination be freer…" (Zaera 1995). He does this in many ways including: sincerely working with and being challenged by the client, through collaboration with other artists and architects, and through a division of the design process into stages that require constant interpretation and translation. The interpretation of the sketches through the models by the project architects, is an example of this. This strategy is similar to the idea of complementarity described by the physicist Neils Bohr where he suggests that the richness of shared experience can only be approached through multiple, overlapping, and mutually exclusive forms of representations.

Some projects begin without Gehry's drawings, such as the Millennium Park Music Pavilion in Chicago, where the singularity of the program allowed for a direct start with the design process model. One of Gehry's early choices for this project was a simple curving roof structure that he felt was sympathetic to the memory of Mies Van de Rohe. Pushed by the desires of the client, the project developed into a more familiar and exuberant form. Other work, such as the Stata Center at MIT involved over fifty drawings by Gehry himself and hundreds of others by the design team.

4.4 Design Process Models: Building a Drawing

> There are those who choose the swampy lowlands. They deliberately involve themselves in messy but crucially important problems and, when asked to describe their methods of inquiry, they speak of experience, trial and error, intuition, and muddling through. (Schon 1983)

The Lewis residence (1986-1995) changed the office. Occurring over ten years, the design of a house in Lindhurst, Ohio for an eccentric client grew from 1700 square meters to over 4000 and back to 2000 square meters. At a projected cost of 80 million dollars (in its largest state), it was 1/8 the size of Bilbao which cost one hundred million dollars. Described by Gehry as the equivalent of a MacArthur genius grant, the project characterizes the various ways the design process models catalyze the design development. With hundreds of models spanning Gehry's formal investigations

Weatherhead School of Management, 1997-, Cleveland, OH, design process models (photo: author).

from fragmented and clustered volumes to intensely organic and curvilinear forms, the unbuilt project formed an immensely rich archive of ideas, and methods. The design work also spanned Gehry's pre, and post, digital adaptations. Gehry credits the origins of the Guggenheim Museum in Bilbao, and the EMP project, to this body of work. The models employ a variety of materials including paper, wood, melted plastic, plaster, metal, and wax infused velvet. At various times the project involved collaborations with architect Phillip Johnson, landscape architect Maggie Keswick Jencks, and artists Larry Bell, Frank Stella, Claes Oldenburg, and Coosje van Bruggen. The work also notably included the development of the *horse's head* that is the only form to date directly generated in the computer (by Gehry). It is the source for the conference room in the DG bank project in Berlin as well as a sculptural commission for the Gagosian Gallery in Los Angeles. The group of design process models for the Lewis residence stands alone as an example of artistic accomplishment of the highest order.

In general, the design process models begin directly over the

Weatherhead School of Management, stack laminate foamcore model (photo: author).

block program models. Starting small and getting bigger, the models are formal, spatial, and material tests of the gestural implications of Gehry's drawings. They employ torn paper, wood, metal mesh, and any other material that has the property to capture the "latent energies" of the drawing. Built quickly, a model a day is not unusual for this intense stage of the process. Sometimes occurring simultaneously with the design of the program models, it is the stage where Gehry himself is most directly involved with the design development. Webb, who calls the process "cooking", describes the interaction between himself and Gehry to be "definitely based on the model", and at more of a "hands-on physical level" than an intellectual one. He describes a joke in the office where a film crew wanted to film the magic moment of the creative ferment and quickly became bored with the grunts, sighs, and gestural communication, as if one of Gehry's drawings had suddenly come alive, expressing acutely the process of "muddling through" (Lindsey 2001).

Typical architectural offices generally confine model building to presentations. In Gehry's office the design process models are built, rebuilt, torn apart, and rebuilt again. Then another one is made. The models test material possibilities, formal arrangements based on the program model configuration, and often entirely new radical directions. If a better direction is uncovered it feeds back into the process and prompts adjustment. Often Gehry will be tearing paper himself. At other times his direction is completely through the drawing, sometimes via fax and videoconference. During this part of a project, Webb, who is often working on several designs at once, gives his entire attention to a single effort. Assisted by a score of young architect model builders who are trying to tap into the flow, they bend, fold, tear, and construct. The models accumulate around the designers like physical manifestations of some mental battle that still rages.

There is a general understanding in the office that after Gehry's close friend, sculptor Richard Serra, visits and talks to Gehry about the development of the current project, the design model will be torn apart the next day. Serra, an astute architectural critic, adds another level of interpretation to Gehry's translation of sketch, to model, to building.

The design process model also operates as a collaborative environment. It facilitates interaction between Gehry and the project architects, and between the design team and the client. It also allows the process to move quickly and explore numerous possibilities and variations, sometimes necessitating a renewed commitment on the part of the client. Gehry states:

> They think I am doing four different schemes. "I like the first one, the second one, I liked the third one - now you're doing it again?" So they think you're pulling the carpet out. Some clients don't understand the process. What I'm telling them is, "I'm bringing you into the process. Watch it, get involved, understand that I'm not stopping here". (Friedman 1991)

4.5 Final Design Model

Painters say that knowing when to stop is an essential aspect of painting. One way to know when to stop is to go too far. Because the model is not the final product, unlike the painting, it is not too late to retreat. As the numerous design process models begin to coalesce into a direction that captures the gesture of the drawings and begin to solve the functional and site relationships, or go too far, a final design model is built. This larger scale model allows for more precise structural development, as well as the development of details relating to cladding, fenestration, and material selection. Often an even larger model will be built to study the primary interior spaces. Model scopes, and photographs, supplement plans and sections, to suggest eye level views and create a sense of being in the space. Gehry states: "We work from the inside out mostly" (Friedman 1991).

In earlier projects the computer would be used only after the development of the final design model. With a limited number of workstations (at the time costing $70,000 a seat) project architects scheduled CATIA time in advance. (Fineout) In more recent projects the computer has begun to impact the development of the design process models. By capturing the surfaces using CATIA at an early stage, the digital model (the office insists that they not be called drawings) can be sectioned and used to produce paper templates that facilitate the construction of the physical models. Through a simple process of stack lamination, a topographic-like assembly can precisely represent a complex three-dimensional form. Cut from Styrofoam sheets, the process is fast and adaptable. They have also experimented with rapid prototyping tech-

Lewis Residence (unbuilt), Lyndhurst, OH, design process models.

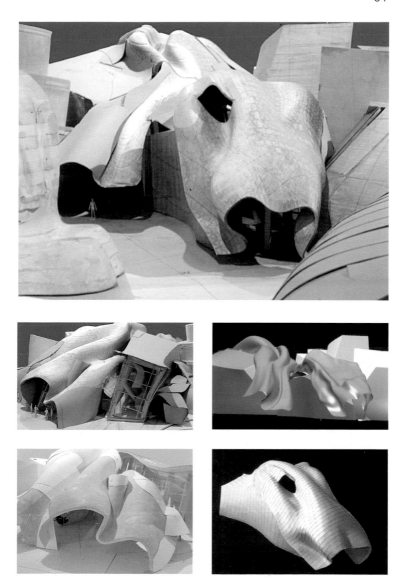

Lewis Residence (unbuilt), Lyndhurst, OH, design process models. CATIA model (all photos except bottom right: author).

niques, where models, and model parts, are produced directly from the digital model. Expensive and time consuming, this step has become reserved for the final verification of the digital model. Called a check model, and done in various techniques, such as stereolithography, and laser cut paper stack models (LOM, laminated object manufacturing), the model is compared to the design model to verify the accuracy of the digital information. This hybrid process with the computer contributing to the design process models allows the precision of the digital model to be supplemented with the tactile feedback of working directly with materials.

It is likely that the role of the computer in the process will continue to be valuable at increasingly earlier stages. It is however, unlikely that it will replace anything. It will simply become an important *part* of the process.

Yet Webb, as well as Gehry, underscores their skepticism of judging forms from the computer screen. Webb states:

> I don't really believe you can see the true shape of an object on a computer screen in two dimensions. I get fooled all the time when we make an object, put it into CATIA and then check it. (Lindsey 2001)

Gehry does not like the way that objects look in the computer and feels that it takes the "juice" out of an idea. He will consciously walk past CATIA stations in the office with diverted eyes so as not to be tempted (Fineout 2001). While he speculates that "the younger kids" will design with it, he prefers to hold the image in his head, through the drawing, through the model, and from the computer back to the model (Friedman 1991).

One strength of a digital model is its capacity to act like something that is between a drawing and a thing. A line in a computer-modeling program can be picked up, moved, and operated on, as if it were an object. Like a drawing, it embodies a level of abstraction that requires perceptual engagement and translation.

Webb states: "The computer makes the process continuous." Marcel Duchamp proposed to call his works delays rather than paintings because they left "temporal distortions" (Willis 1999). They freeze time and action into a solid state that can be contemplated and checked. The physical models exist as a "hole" with a particular "aura". They are the opposite of the computer model

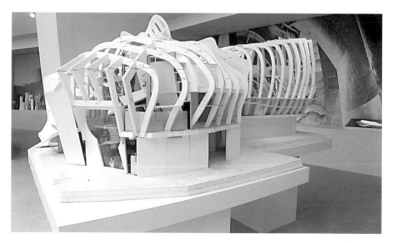

Final Design Models. Top: Disney Concert Hall Los Angeles, CA, 1987-. Middle: DG Bank, 1995-2001, Berlin, Germany (photo: author). Bottom: EMP, Seattle, WA, 1995-2000 (photo: author).

Ray and Maria Stata Center,1998- MIT, Cambridge, MA, program models, design process models. Bottom right: final design model.

which is the next step in the process. The computer model becomes provisionally dynamic by *processing time*. Gehry states:

> It takes a long time. It is like watching paint dry, and I will move things. Sometimes it goes too far, and then we pull it back... I want to go back and recall things so we can rebuild. (Friedman 1991)

The "delay" of the physical model is countered with the *processed time* of the digital model resulting in a fluent dialogue.

4.6 Digitizing

Once the final design model is complete it is translated into a digital model through digitizing. The office is always checking out the latest equipment and currently uses a FARO digitizer, designed to map the vertebrae of the spine in preparation for surgery. Resembling a nineteenth century invention, the pantograph, used to copy drawings and objects, the digitizer produces lines and curves corresponding to points on the model. This correspondence between a physical point, and a virtual point in the computer, is at the heart of the digitizing process. The points are generated in several different stages. Generally the first stage involves drawing waterlines on the model at equal intervals as if the model is being translated into a topography model. These lines are then traced with the digitizer. Another method begins with locating the extreme boundary points of the model and then tracing the edges of major curves. If a surface is a rule-developed surface – a surface that can be flattened to form a plane without compressing or stretching – the rule lines can be traced. A third method involves the tracing of a grid superimposed on the model. The

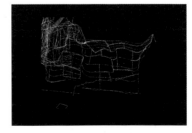

Digitizing a model from the EMP project into CATIA with a FARO digitizer.

intersection points of the grid are then digitized. In general: waterlines and grids describe the flow or curve direction; ruling lines and edges describe features. By digitizing both flow and feature, the physical model is translated into a digital model.

Depending on the complexity of the physical model, any and all of these methods may be employed. For a particularly complex model of a flower shaped fountain for the Disney Concert Hall, a CAT Scan (computed axial tomography) machine was used. Located in the Heart Center at UCLA, this machine is typically used to produce detailed cross sectional images of the brain. The rotating x-ray devise produced precise images of sections taken through the physical model. The sequential section images were then transferred to an image editing software and combined into a three-dimensional digital model.

This technique, although extremely expensive, holds promise for future use as a model digitizer.

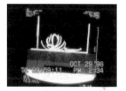

Scanning of DCH model to obtain sectional data

bebel reconstruction of DCH fountain with sections

Disney Concert Hall Fountain. Top: CAT scanning. Bottom: physical model and Froebel method reconstruction of sections.

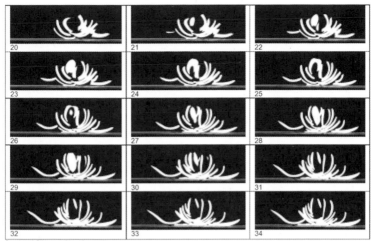

Sectional Slices at 3mm intervals

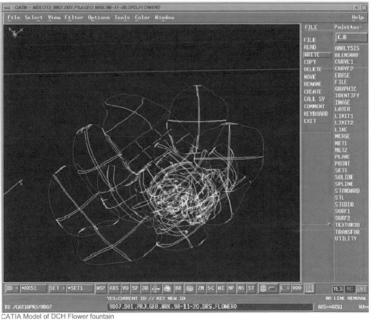

CATIA Model of DCH Flower fountain

Top: CAT scan sections. Bottom: CATIA model.

4.7 Closing the Form

Once the points, which generally describe curves, are established
in the digital model, a surface is created that attempts to coincide
with the points. This laborious process must resolve the points
into a form that "closes", or in the language of another modeling
software, becomes a "well-formed object". It is a process familiar
to surveyors who, when describing a property survey with dis-
tances and angles, must close the perimeter to a specified level of
accuracy. Closing also involves subtle adjustments of the surfaces
as well as an understanding of plane and non-Euclidean geometry. Some surface functions in CATIA are named after the mathe-
maticians that invented the method of describing and generating
the surface. This process of developing the surface in CATIA was
initially done by "super senior aerospace guys" with extensive
experience. It more recently has become more pervasive throughout the office. As the software has become more affordable and
easier to use, the number of people in the office that use it has
increased. Another three-dimensional modeling software named
RHINO is becoming prevalent, especially for early design process
model development. Dennis Shelden, an associate in Gehry's

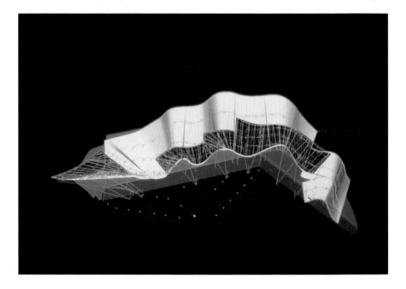

Surface Development in CATIA for the EMP project.

office, whose business card reads Director of Computing, calls the process *advanced surfacing*. Shelden describes this moment in the process to be "mythical", where

> you've got this messy three-dimensional physical model with bondo and paper and little things flying off it. And then you've got a messy construction world where there's concrete, and slop, and it's raining, then somewhere between is this computer process taking some of the looseness out by incorporating analytical techniques and economic considerations, all trying to keep this very free and crazy process on track. And that's what's really great… (Lindsey 2000)

4.8 Rationalization / Legitimization

Usually three digital models are produced: a surface model, describing the exterior surface, a wire frame geometry model, usually describing the structural grid and organization, and an interior surface model. When required the surface model will be further developed to study the patterning of the skin design. The wire frame geometry model forms the basis for the CATIA master model, which becomes the "single source of information" for the project. Coinciding with this development, a process occurs which Glymph calls rationalization. Members of the design team use the term in two ways. In its general use (by Glymph), rationalization describes the process of converting the complex physical models, with all of their indeterminacy, into a digital model where the complexity is tamed through mathematical description. It introduces "rules of constructability" into forms. This also has the effect of legitimizing the "crazy process". The legitimization occurs for a number of reasons, not the least of which is the

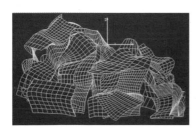

Telluride Residence, Telluride, CO, 1996. Surface development in CATIA.

complete dimensional, as well as three-dimensional control of the digital model. The value of this was well known to Gehry when, in earlier projects, contractors would give astronomical bids for construction because they were unsure of how to build the complex forms. Legitimization also happens because the digital model can be subjected to further scrutiny using technology. Another reason is subtler. Through our belief in the objectivity of technology and science, when something is *measured*, it becomes tangible – even those things that resist measurement. In an ironic reciprocity, similar to the way that the ability to computationally control complexity has allowed Gehry's drawings to be more gestural, the specificity and accuracy of the digital model is balanced by the possibility for greater emphemerality in the completed building. Due to the precise constraint of digital lofting, the building becomes freer.

In the specific sense, rationalization is using the capability of the computer to generate area and volume calculations which allow the model to be evaluated through what, in another era, was called value engineering. Value engineering is essentially a process

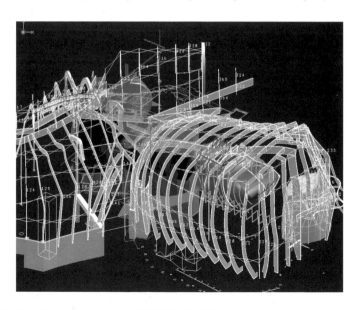

Structural frame development in CATIA for the EMP project.

that uses function cost analysis to reduce cost. Usually done after the design work is complete, it often results in large-scale cuts in program, quality, or complexity. In Gehry's office, occurring during the entire design development, it is used to rationalize the form relative to cost, complexity, material, and structural considerations. The process involves translating the architectural elements, skin panels, beams, columns, etc., into the following hierarchy: straight, flat, curved, doubly curved, and warped (highly shaped), each representing a higher cost. The translation continues through the following syntax: repetitive, similar, and unique, again each representing a higher cost of manufacture and assembly. With the cost of digitally driven manufacturing based on machine time, rather than labor costs, similar pieces can be made as cheaply as repetitive parts, because they represent a similar amount of time. The design team uses a rule-of-thumb that keeps the highly shaped pieces to five percent (Macleod 1993). Gehry, speaking now with experience in constructing his forms, states:

> Flat pieces cost one dollar, single curvature pieces cost two dollars; double curvature pieces cost ten dollars. The good thing about the computer is that it allows you to keep a close control over the geometry and the budget. It was not just speculation; it was real. (Zaera 1995)

Another specific procedure of rationalization involves the use of modified Gaussian Analysis. The procedure evaluates the degree of compound curvature of building components, particularly surface panels and skins, using a set of mathematical functions. The degree of curvature, coupled with a particular material's behavioral properties, can be represented in a three-dimensional digital model, allowing problem areas to be identified. If the color coded digital model shows that the material will not bend in that way, modifications can

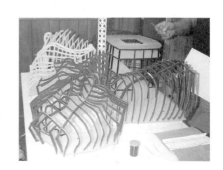

Structural frame model for the EMP project.

72

be made. If the analysis shows that the curvature is within the material's limits, but still highly "shaped" – a more expensive condition – a determination can be made as to the necessary action. The process of Gaussian analysis, which began with the Guggenheim Museum in Bilbao, was used extensively in the EMP project resulting in a construction contract that stipulated the maximum area of highly shaped areas. Augmented by extensive physical mock-ups and tests, this process has now become a part of the *expertise of complex curvilinearity* of the design and fabrication teams.

Two techniques in development promise to greatly contribute to the rationalization process. The design for the composition of the metal surface shingles in the EMP project utilized generative shape grammar algorithms. A shape grammar, which has its origin in formal grammars, is a rule-based system that can be used for composition. Numerous examples can be generated directly from the rules, testing a variety of conditions. Employed and coded by Shelden, and used in the EMP project to study efficient and aesthetic ways for laying out the aluminum shingles, spatial grammars have the capacity to use the information of the digital

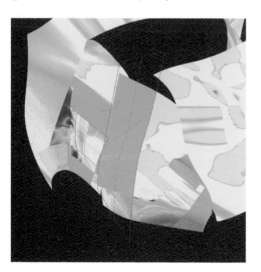

model in a way that extends the number of variations that the designer may evaluate. They may also include rules that provide combinations of evaluation criteria that would be too complex to evaluate in more traditional ways.

Shelden, who is working on his Ph.D. in Design and Computation at

Gaussian analysis in CATIA for the EMP project, red indicates problem area.

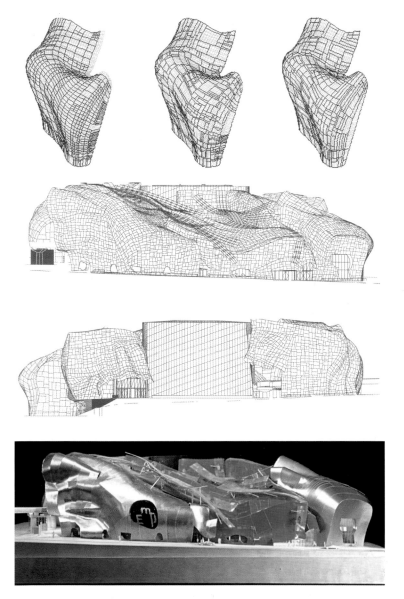

Top: Shape Grammar algorithm panel variations. Middle: front and rear elevations. Bottom: final design model.

MIT, is also "developing the future". Paper surfaces, it turns out, are not simple. A small area may contain 10-12 developable surfaces, along with areas that are indeterminate. Writing a program that uses finite-element analysis to simulate the spatial behavior of curving forms, Shelden is working to make the *materials* of the design process models truly digital. With this capability, the embedded information of the shape informs the mathematics of the surfaces directly through the digital model. The digital model provides a kind of material (tactile) feedback. The surfaces become intelligent.

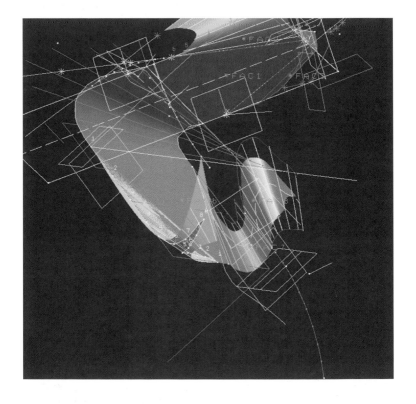

Digital paper surface generated using a new program developed by Dennis Shelden.

5. Digital (Information) Diversity

Digital information is malleable. Once the information of the final design model is in a digital form, it can play a number of other roles; simulation, direct detailing, and computer aided manufacturing (CAM), being the most recent. While Smith recites an office rule, "model all and only necessary design information", the digital models have become increasingly more detailed. This occurs through the continued development of the model by the design team, as well as contributions by consultants and manufacturers who relay their work back. Shelden describes this part of the process to be fraught with translation difficulties between various softwares and formats, in some cases requiring ingenious translation *kludges* written by Shelden. He describes a future where the entire building is constructed in the computer, much like the fabled design and construction of the Boeing 767. The difference, he points out, is the 767 is built in a building, and the building is built on a construction site (Lindsey 2000).

5.1 Simulation

Throughout design development, simulations using the digital model and physical model are used to evaluate a number of important issues. For the Disney Concert Hall, acoustic testing was done with the digital model and a large-scale physical model. Fine-tuning of the room through an evaluation of reverberation times was accomplished using laser targeting, and real musicians. Physical models constructed using information from the digital model are routinely used for wind tunnel testing of the curving forms. Due to compound curvatures, single roof panels in the EMP project may be exposed to both positive and negative pressures. To study this, Wallace Engineering used Multiframe software to conduct digital wind load simulations on groups of panels described in the digital model (Lin 2000). Sun studies showing shadow movement and the shading of exterior spaces are done using CATIA's rendering module. The changing lighting conditions that happen throughout a day can be evaluated in this manner. This, along with digital and analogue wind studies, was very important in the development of the courtyard space for the Stata Center project at MIT. For the design of the atrium in the Weatherhead School of

Management project in Cleveland, computational fluid-dynamic modeling was used to study the flow of air in a potential fire.

While Gehry eschews the term "green" as a designation, he does use intelligent siting, and massing, as well as computer simulations to make his buildings as environmentally conscious as possible. Use of the digital model after construction, and during the normal operations of the building's life span, allows energy management to be tracked and optimized. In this way the *digital life* of the building contributes to its on-going physical life.

The digital design information can also be used for direct analysis and detailing of structural elements. Finite-element analysis used by structural engineering programs allows for direct calculation of forces, and member sizing, for complex shapes. This is a significant advance that has contributed to Gehry's formal inventiveness. Using the geometry model as a source, structural steel detailing software can generate a visually and dimensionally accurate digital

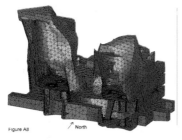

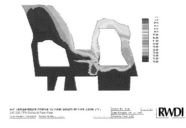

Top: wind tunnel test model for the Disney Concert Hall, Bottom: fluid thermal, dynamics modeling for the Weatherhead School of Management atrium.

model of the steel frame – right down to the bolt. Glymph describes a recent use of this capability where Capco, a steel fabricator in Rhode Island, using software called SDS, generated shop drawings from a digital model in three hours. A similar software, X-Steel, is being used on the Disney Concert Hall. Traditional techniques of shop drawing production in Autocad would have taken several months. The computer-generated drawings, which are detailed down to the length of the weld, allowed very precise construction estimates based on known, rather than estimated, production time. Glymph points out a surprising fact; the cost of producing and reviewing shop drawings in a large project far exceeds the architectural and engineering fees (Cocke 2000).

Another use for a deep digital model (one that includes three-dimensional representations of all major elements) is the coordination of the various building systems. Electrical, mechanical, and plumbing consultants (EMP) are usually one of the last to join the design team, making the coordination of the pipes and ducts very

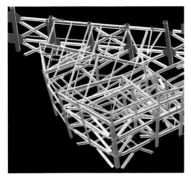

Top: sun studies for MIT Stata Center project. Bottom: steel frame model for the Disney concert Hall, steel frame under construction.

difficult. Using the digital model for coordination, the placement of these elements can be done so that they do not run into each other. It also allows for a unified strategy for the integration of all systems. These systems routinely comprise 40-60% of a building's budget. When they can contribute to the building's expression and conceptual clarity, they become both functional and beautiful. Shelden describes the digital model for the Disney Concert Hall to be one of the most complete that the office has produced. While he jokes that, there is a lot of time spent checking that ducts do not coincide with beams, the potential is that this work will become a common part of the coordination allowed by the digital model.

Several important coordination issues for the EMP project were addressed using the digital model. "Hiking trails", required by code for roof access, were designed, and developed within the curving landscape-like forms of the building using the CATIA model. In addition, the exterior aluminum skin is not a water barrier and required the design and placement of numerous gutters and rain leaders. Threaded between the skin and the sprayed concrete shell of the building, the digital model allowed these elements to be coordinated with a high degree of precision. This would have required numerous drawings of the structure in progress had traditional methods been employed.

5.2 Computer Aided Manufacturing

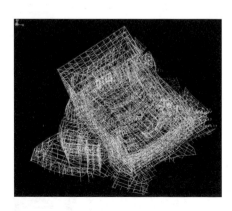

Perhaps the most radical (elaborate) use of the digital information is in directing the actual construction of the components of a building. As Webb describes the design process to be continuous through the digital model, computer aided manufacturing allows the continuity to extend from design through construction. This continuity crosses traditional professional

Structural Steel wire frame model in CATIA for the Disney Concert Hall.

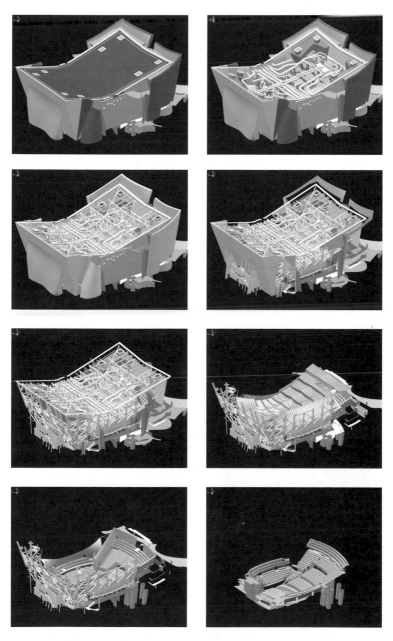

Systems model in CATIA for the Disney Concert Hall.

boundaries, and practices, reconstituting the architect in a central role in the process of construction. For architecture, it promises to be as important an influence as the adaptation of industrial practices over the last fifty years. Mass production, standardization, prefabrication, and the industrial production of building components have changed the design of buildings into a process of building component selection and arrangement (Ruby). These practices have changed the role of the contractor into one of management and assembly. With the opportunities offered through "mass-customization", the traditional rules of economy, where regular organizations and straight repetitive elements cost less, are no longer operative. While assembly is still required by the contractor, the continuity of the process allows for the manufacturer and the contractor to be a part of the design team as a significant partner.

This process is beautifully illustrated in Gehry's Zollhof complex in Düsseldorf, Germany (1994-1999). The typical design process resulted in a digital model that described Gehry's design intentions. While all three buildings ("father, child and mother") have a rhythmic shape, the brick building is the most angular, and the metal the most fluid. All three were constructed with a concrete frame, floors, and load-bearing walls, to avoid what the client termed "the wrapped up roller-coaster" appearance of a curtain wall facade (Nicolin 1998). The center building was clad in precast concrete panels. The panels were made utilizing CNC (computer numerical control) routers, which cut Styrofoam molds that were then fitted with reinforcing steel and poured with concrete. The 2.4-meter-wide by 3.4-meter-high by 0.9-meter-thick milled blanks were then recycled. The 355 concrete panels, each different, were assembled and the undulating shape emerged as a result of the direct translation of digital data into physical material. The 1600 operable windows, each with a specific interface detail, were also coordinated using the digital model.

This process has been extended in the DG Bank Building (1995-2001) in Berlin; an 18,000 square meter corporate headquarters for DG Bank next to the Brandenberg Gate. In addition to the offices, the project includes thirty-three units of housing, a conference center, a cafeteria, and large lecture hall. The five to ten story courtyard building is the result of a winning competition entry by Gehry. In the development of the final design model Gehry had yet to decide on the crucial element to be located in

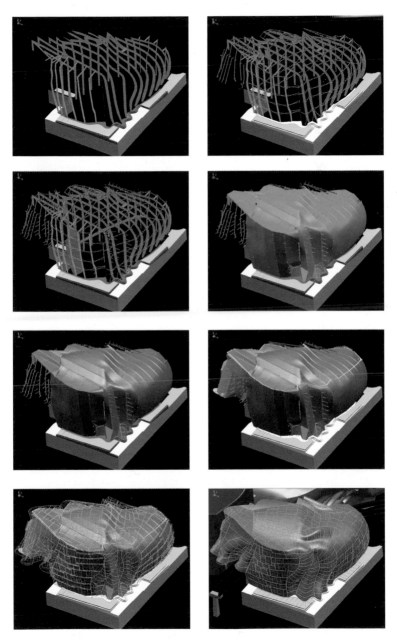

Structure and skin development in CATIA for the EMP project.

the glass enclosed courtyard. Trying several odd model pieces lying around the studio, including boat and fish shaped elements, he chose a model of the horse head piece that had been done for the Lewis Residence, thinking that he could change it later. He won the competition for, among other things, the location of an object in the courtyard that would later become the conference center. The clients loved the horse head. So did Gehry. He states:

> We made it better, because it was something we'd appropriated from somewhere else - which we don't do that often... I loved the shape. So I changed it. (Friedman 1991)

The stainless steel clad horse's head conference room is one of the few shapes that Gehry has built using stretched and compressed metal panels. Other projects rely simply on the ability of metal to bend. The compound curves of the horse head are built much like the body of car. Using information from the digital model, 306 Styrofoam molds were milled using CNC routers. These molds were transported to the Czech Republic where they were used to cast 32 matching cast iron forms. The forms were shipped to Sweden where flat stainless steel panels at a final thickness of 4 millimeters were heated to 1,815 degrees Celsius. Using a 1,500 metric ton press fitted with the cast iron form the panels were pressed into their final compound shape and assembled around a curving steel frame. The interior of the conference center is beau-

Der Neue Zollhof, Düsseldorf, Germany, 1994-99 (photo: Thomas Mayer).

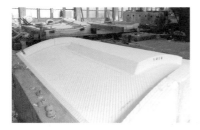

Top: CNC routers cutting foam blocks. Middle: foam form and precast concrete elements. Bottom: cast-in-place wall using foam forms, window installation (photos: Thomas Mayer).

tifully detailed, using Douglas Fir strips, and adds to the distinction of the wood-lined courtyard to the stone clad exterior.

All offices open into the seven-story wood-lined courtyard each with a spectacular view of the horse head conference center. German structural engineer Jorg Schlaich, who Gehry describes as the best in the world, designed the fish shaped glass roof. Four cable trusses that connect to concrete piers at eight locations support the 150 metric ton glass and stainless steel roof. After rejecting a thick and bulky solution proposed by another engineer, the final form is the result of studying a number of different variations – the final solution defying gravity with the gesture of a swelling cloud. Gehry states how this fluent process is changing the craft of building:

> This technology provides a way for me to get closer to the craft. In the past, there were many layers between my rough sketch and the final building, and the feeling of the design could get lost before it reached the craftsman. It feels like I've been speaking a foreign language, and now, all of a sudden, the craftsman understands me. In this case, the computer is not dehumanizing; it's an interpreter. (Gehry, CATIA)

For the EMP project, CNC guided plasma cutters were used to cut the flanges of the curving structural steel members, many of which were over forty feet long. Computer controlled rolling machines were used to bend the flanges and an automated trolley, which ran along the flange, welded the assembly together. Fabricated by the company Olympia Wire, a veteran steel worker states: "The steel ribs are curves of the 11th order meaning there

DG Bank, interior courtyard with horse head conference center, nearing completion (photo: Craig Webb).

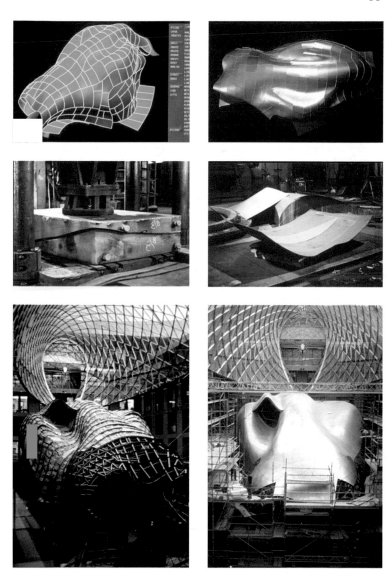

Top: CATIA model, physical model. Middle: hydraulic forming of skin panels. Bottom: horse head under construction (photo top right: Joshua White, middle and bottom Tensho Takemoni).

is no true radius. Not only are no two of the building's 239 ribs alike, there's no two feet alike" (Gragg 1999). Accurate placement and alignment of the ribs, no small task for a building where typical destinations such as wall, roof, beam, and column are blurred, was accomplished using laser positioning and surveying equipment. These techniques, which will become more typical, and will begin to include global positioning satellite information, extend the depth of the digital model into the construction site.

In addition to the manufacture of the structural members in the EMP project, CATIA information was used to produce a developed template of each of the 21,000 stainless steel and aluminum skin shingles, which were assembled into 4,800 prefabricated panels. Zahner Sheet Metal Company, the contractor for the panels, required 250mb of computer memory to define the characteristics of a single panel. This structural topography of panels results in a building with 13,000 square meters of floor space while having over 22,000 square meters of roof.

The curving steel structure of the EMP is punctuated with hundreds of pedestals that resolve the difference in geometry between the structure and the skin. These pedestals vary in length from several inches to eight feet. Splines, which support the roof panels, are attached to the pedestals using a pivoting ball and socket joint reminiscent of the uni-strut connector used in the Bilbao Guggenheim. These connectors became known as the "rock-n-roll joint". The 2,700 rock-n-roll joints allowed for finetuning of the skin to the structure assembly. Using large wrenches, and guided by radio communication, the workmen, in a process described as "herding sheep", adjusted the panel joints to within three-thousandths of an inch. At the height of the construction for EMP there were as many as ten CATIA stations operating between the various construction contractors. One of these contractors states:"You can make all the decisions and fix the mistakes while it's still electrons" (Gragg 1999).

5.3 C-cubed

Consultants for Gehry's projects are increasingly using CATIA, in part supported by a computer consulting company, C-cubed, Virtual Architecture, Inc., formed by Rick Smith. Supporting the work on the digital model in Gehry's office, C-cubed also facilitates the use of CATIA with the increasing number of consultants, manufacturers, and contractors that work with Gehry's office. Working in a consulting capacity allows Smith freedom to operate between the architect and the contractor. Smith's provisional role as a consultant to Gehry's office was originally due to a skepticism of technology. Now it is a specific management strategy that allows his company to assist the other partners without affecting their autonomy. This also has important liability advantages for both Gehry and Smith.

Smith also has other clients. Using his early experience in shipbuilding, Smith has worked with sculptor Richard Serra on his Torqued Ellipse series. Using CATIA to help refine Serra's physical models, and to direct the fabrication of the large steel forms, Smith has used the digital model to bridge art and technology. CATIA allows a complex curving form to be developed into a flat shape. The program determines the precise multiple lines, along which the sheet of steel must be bent, to correctly form the curving shape. Working with equipment used to produce enormous ship hulls, the steel is literally pleated, rather than rolled, to produce the elegant final structure. Another work by Serra, The Snake, is a permanent installation in the Guggenheim Bilbao. Gehry, pointing to Serra's piece in the large gallery emotionally describes the curves of his building as crude in comparison to the curves of Serra's Snake.

The success of these partnerships, and the use of CATIA software in general, is measured in part by the fact that many of the companies who work with Gehry's office, and with Rick Smith, never work in the same way again. Seeing the value of the digital model and CATIA's role in generating and managing it, they are also changing the game. Glymph warns that this will happen without the architect if they are slow to change their paperbound traditions (Cocke 2000).

5.4 Master Model / Master Builder

The master CATIA model is the "single source of information" for the design of the building and becomes a legal part of the contract documents. While it may eventually take many forms, its base condition is a wire frame, three-dimensional database from which all dimensional information can be extracted. Glymph envisions this model, and CATIA, to allow the architect to become a coordinator of information between the various groups involved in the construction of the building. The model can allow the architect to com-

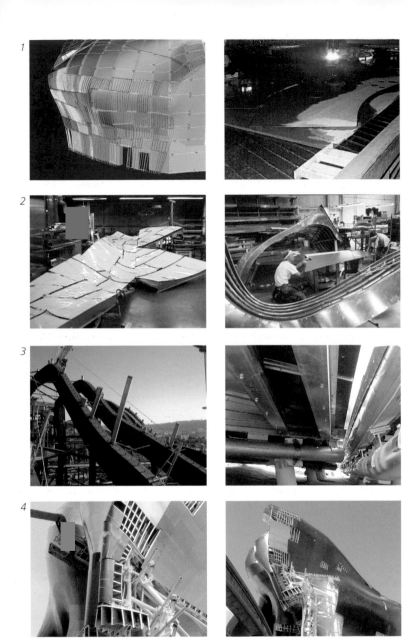

EMP project, 1.CATIA model panel development, CNC plasma cutting of beam flanges, 2. pre-fabricated skin panels, 3. pedestals, rock-n-roll joint. 4. skin & structure (photo: author).

municate precise information for the design to the contractors and manufacturers, and they in turn, communicate their technical requirements and cost information back – the final stage being the direct manufacture of the building components from the digital data (Novitski 1992). Often with over one hundred separate companies involved in a large-scale construction project, uniting the players through one modeling system would overcome the dispersion of responsibility that has led to difficulties in management. Ultimately, allowing for all communications to involve only digital information, the model could signal a significant reduction in drawing sets, shop drawings, and specifications. This is already reflected in the office's current practices where the CATIA model generally takes precedence (legal as well as in practice) over the construction document set. This is a significant change in standard practice where specifications take precedence over drawings and specified dimensions are subject to site verification. This paper-less process has already occurred to some extent in the EMP project, where a client interested in technology, Paul Allen, and a short construction schedule, saw information moving directly from the digital model to the fabricator and then to the construction site. Glymph states that, "both time and money can be eliminated from the construction process by shifting the design responsibility forward" (Cocke 2000). Along with this responsibility comes increased liability. When the architect supplies a model that is shared, and becomes the single source of information, the distributed liability of current architectural practice is changed. This is compounded through electronic dialog which blurs lines of responsibilities (Novitski 1992). This increased liability has been a difficult problem to address, especially when the stance of architectural professional organizations, and insurance companies, has pushed architects to minimize their liability. The American Institute of Architects (AIA) has recommended that the architect play an observational role in construction and allow the contractor to be responsible for all building issues. Glymph realizes that the expertise needs to "stay where it belongs" but the master model puts the architect at the center of the process using digital tools to become the master builder. Gehry states:

> For what it is worth, I think the younger generation ought to consider becoming the master builders again, taking over the parental role in the construction process,... (Jencks 1995)

A Fluent Practice

Fluent, from the Latin *fluere*, to flow, describes Gehry's emergent process of sketch, to model, to building. This strange and wonderful process has become almost as well known as his architecture. The models precede the buildings in publicity, as well as time, and influence the experience of the real thing. Few visit the Guggenheim in Bilbao without having read the book, or seen it on Charlie Rose. His use of the computer has, in a strange way, allowed a (digital) narrative to emerge that connects the process of designing, the process of construction, to the life of his buildings, and the people who use them. Drawings, models (still lifes), courageous clients, and talented partners, populate the narrative. Images on screens have become media as well as medium. His later work has become complex and self-organizing. Candice Bergen visits his office.

The physical models have been augmented with digital ones that contribute to the fluency, and re-organize the possibilities. Gehry's belief in the building is supported through a paradox where the instrumental role of representations is countered with skepticism of their ability to envision the building. The computer has deepened the skepticism and allowed the representations to become more powerful. Malcolm McCullough in his book *Abstracting Craft* states that computers allow us to work on abstractions as if they are things, and inhabit representations as if they are spaces. The computer has allowed Gehry's drawings to be built.

The history of digital tools' influence in architectural practice was first in drafting, then in visualization, and now construction. The digital model allows the design information to become construction information. Construction, once a significant technological, and cultural activity, has become a commodity like many other activities. The building of cathedrals or the raising of barns notwithstanding, construction rarely develops community and embodies progress as it once did. The concept of the master builder is not a nostalgic hope for lost power so much as a belief that buildings and the processes by which they are built can become as significant as the influence they play in our built environment. In his acceptance of the Pritzker Prize, Gehry states:

Our problems as architects increase in complexity as time goes on. We have difficulty with the art of city building. We are finding ways of working together, artists and architects, architects and architects, clients and architects. The dream is that each brick, each window, each wall, each road, each tree, will be placed lovingly by craftsman, client, architect, and people to create beautiful cities.

References

Arnell, Peter, Bickford, Ted, *Frank Gehry, Buildings and Projects*, Rizzoli International Publications, New York, NY 1985.

Van Bruggen, Coosje, *Frank O. Gehry, The Guggenheim Museum Bilbao*, Guggenheim Foundation, New York 1997.

Dal Co, Francesco, Forester, Kurt W., *Frank O. Gehry The Complete Works*, Monacelli Press, New York 1998.

Forster, Kurt W., *Frank O. Gehry*, Cantz, Berlin 1999.

Friedman, Mildred (ed.), *Gehry Talks: architecture + process*, Rizzoli, New York 1991.

Gougeon Brothers, *The Gougeon Brothers on Boat Construction*, Pendel Printing, Midland, Michigan 1979.

Jencks, Charles (ed.), *Robert Maxwell, Jeffrey Kipnis. Frank O. Gehry Individual Imagination and Cultural Conservatism*, Academy Editions, London 1995.

Harbeson, John F., *The Study of Architectural Design*, The Pencil Point Press, New York 1926

Kubler, George, *The Shape of Time: Remarks on the History of Things*, Yale University Press, New Haven, CT 1962.

McCullough, Malcolm, *Abstracting Craft, The Practised Digital Hand*, The MIT Press, Cambridge, Mass. 1996.

Saggio, Antonino, *Frank O. Gehry. Architetture residuali*, Testo & Immagine, Torino 1997

Schon, Donald A., *The Reflective Practitioner: How Professionals Think in Action*, HarperCollins, New York, NY 1983.

Schama, Simon, *Landscape Memory*, Knopf, New York 1995.

Walker Art Center, *The Architecture of Frank Gehry*, Rizzoli 1986

Willis, Daniel, *The Emerald City and Other Essays on the Architectural Imagination*, Princeton Architectural Press, New York 1999.

CATIA at Frank O. Gehry & AMP Associates, Inc,
http://www-3.ibm.com/solutions/engineering/esindus.nsf/Public/sufran

Cocke, Andrew, "The Business of Complex Curves", in *Architecture*, December 2000.

Ivy, Robert, "Frank Gehry: Plain Talk with a Master, in *Architectural Record*, May 1999.

Gragg, Randy, "Museum Design Tests Hoffman's learning Curve", in *The Oregonian*, April 11, 1999.

Lin, Charles, "Creating Sleek Metal Skins for Buildings", in *Architectural Record*, October, 2000.

Lecuyer, Annette, "Art Gallery, Bilbao, Spain", in *Architectural Review*, December 1997.

MacLeod, Douglas, "Gehry's Choice", in *Canadian Architect*, July, 1993.

Nicolin, Pierluigi, "The Dismemberment of Orpheus," in *Lotus International*, no. 98, 1998.

Novitski, B.J., "Gehry Forges New computer Links," in *Architecture*, August 1992.

Pehnt, Wolfgang, "The New Zollhof in Dusseldorf," in *Domus*, October 1999.

Zaera, Alejandro, "Frank Gehry 1991-5, Conversations with Frank O. Gehry", in *El Croquis*, no. 74-5, 1995.

Beucker, Thomas, *Digital Real*, "Der Neue Zollhof, Düsseldorf"
http://www.a-matter.de/digital-real/eng/iedefault.htm
Ruby, Andreas, *Digital Real*, "Architecture in the Age of Digital Producibility,"
http://www.a-matter.de/digital-real/eng/iedefault.htm
Fineout, Matt, conversations with Fineout, April-July 2001
Lindsey, Bruce, conversations with Craig Webb, Dennis Shelden, Rick Smith, November 3, 2000

Fluent Practice: I owe the use of this phrase to Bill Sharpel of SHoP, a young New York based architecture firm. Bill describes Gehry's use of computers in construction as influential to their digitally adapted practice. They are also changing the game.

INTERNET SITES:
http://www-3.ibm.com/solutions/engineering/esindus.nsf/Public/sufran
http://www.baunetz.de/arch/archplus/30461c__.htm
http://www.sitesarch.org/reviews/GehryStudy/AStudy.html
http://www.sitesarch.org/reviews/GehryBil.html
http://www.archrecord.com/CONTEDUC/ARTICLES/10_00_2.asp
http://www.designarchitecture.com/view_article.cfm?aid=228&return=articles.cfm
http://www.guggenheim-bilbao.es/frances/home.htm
http://www.guggenheim.org/exhibitions/gehry/index.html
http://web.mit.edu/buildings/statacenter/construction.htm
http://weatherhead.cwru.edu/lewis/lewis.shtml
http://www.arcspace.com/gehry_new/index.html

For a history of CATIA see: *http://www.dsweb.com/*
For information on the program see:
http://www.d-digest.com/catiadigitaldigest/CDDArchive/V1I20CDD.html#News

All images courtesy of Frank Gehry Partners LLP, unless noted.

The Information Technology Revolution in Architecture
is a new series reflecting on the effects the virtual
dimension is having on architects and architecture in
general. Each volume will examine a single topic, high-
lighting the essential aspects and exploring their rele-
vance for the architects of today.

Series edited by **Antonino Saggio**

Other titles in this series:

Information Architecture
Basis and Future of CAAD
Gerhard Schmitt
ISBN 3-7643-6092-5

HyperArchitecture
Spaces in the Electronic Age
Luigi Prestinenza Puglisi
ISBN 3-7643-6093-3

Digital Eisenman
An Office of the Electronic Era
Luca Galofaro
ISBN 3-7643-6094-1

Digital Stories
The Poetics of Communication
Maia Engeli
ISBN 3-7643-6175-1

Virtual Terragni
CAAD in Historical and Critical Research
Mirko Galli / Claudia Mühlhoff
ISBN 3-7643-6174-3

Natural Born CAADesigners
Young American Architects
Christian Pongratz / Maria Rita Perbellini
ISBN 3-7643-6246-4